Siddur

Siddur

Since the beginning of biblical days, prayer has been an important part of the Jewish community. Perhaps the oldest fixed prayer is the Shema, which consists of three parts: Deuteronomy 6:4-9, 11:13-21 and Numbers 15:37-41. This prayer was recited twice a day, as instructed in Deuteronomy 6:7: When you lie down and when you get up."

The SIDDUR (prayer book) with fixed prayers structured in a predetermined order, emerged in the eighth century C.E. in Babylon and was first widely published in the ninth century C.E. In traditional Jewish worship, the SIDDUR is built around three daily prayer services, which reflect the three daily offerings in the temple. Incorporated within the SIDDUR is the framework for weekly reading of the Torah and the Nevi' im (Prophets). The SIDDUR is filled with prayers based on Scripture, including the Exodus and AKEDAH ('binding of Isaac") motifs, and the penitential cries and the praises of King David found throughout the Psalms. Messianic prayers also dot the SIDDUR with emphasis on the "horn" and "salvation of David." These prayer books continue to be employed in synagogues in all branches of Judaism throughout the world.

The Messianic Movement is not shy about employing standardized prayer books today in their worship services. Most Messianic synagogues that use these books adopt a Messianic SIDDUR that centralizes Yeshua within its prayer schema. Although following the order of the traditional SIDDUR, they alter some of the prayers and expand on others to stay close to renewed covenant Scripture. Some include the

AVINU ("Our Father") constructed by Yeshua, which is believed by some scholars to be an early outline of the AMIDAH ("Standing Prayer"), a central prayer within the SIDDUR, which includes nineteen thanksgivings and blessings to Elohim.

This is my version (Broken Road Ministries) of the SIDDUR.

"If you keep your feet from breaking the Sabbath and from doing as you please on my holy day, if you call the Sabbath a delight and the LORD's holy day honorable, and if you honor it by not going your own way and not doing as you please or speaking idle words, then you will find your joy in the LORD, and I will cause you to ride in triumph on the heights of the land and to feast on the inheritance of your father Jacob." The mouth of the LORD has spoken.

- Isaiah 58:13-14

Frequently asked questions

Who is a Jew?

In traditional Judaism, one is either a Jew by birth or by choice. For a Jew by birth, there are two basic positions matrilineal (that is, a person is Jewish if born from a Jewish mother) and patrilinieal (born of a Jewish father). Orthodox and Conservative Judaism hold to a matrilineal position. In Reform and Reconstructionist Judaism, a bi-lineal approach is used, acknowledging both matrilineal and patrilineal descent. The Messianic Movement uses the bi-lineal approach.

Generally, all of Judaism traces its origin to Avraham (Abraham), who was called a Hebrew, his son, Yitz' chak (Isaac), and grandson Ya' akov (Jacob). The etymology of the word Jew goes back to the word Y' hudah (Judah), one of the twelve sons of Ya' akov or the twelve tribes of Israel. The root Hebrew meaning of the word Jew (Yehudi) means "to praise." The term "Jew" came to mean anyone from the tribe of Y' hudah. Eventually, it was extended to any of the religion of Judaism (scattered in exile).

But what about Romans 2:28-29? Was Sha' ul (Paul) redefining the term "Jew" only spiritually and thereby rejecting the physical? On the surface it seems so, but when the text is considered with other related verses, it's clear that his purpose was to remind those who were Jews not to rely only upon the physical signs of circumcision, their Jewishness, to be justified before Elohim, but to rely upon the circumcision of the heart that leads to true praise.

Here, at Broken Road Ministries we avoid the term "Messianic Judaism," for several reasons. It paints a false picture, creating confusion for many who come to the Messianic Movement. It gives the impression that the Messianic Movement is Judaism (and that the only difference is our belief in the Messiah). This could not be any more, wrong. Judaism adheres to the ORAL TORAH and follows many man-made laws that YHWH never commanded. Some of these traditions were rejected by Yeshua. If everyone did as 'Yeshua did,' there would be one movement.

Did Yeshua follow some of the Jewish traditions?

Several examples from Yeshua's life illustrate His approach to "the Jewish traditions." A significant passage is Luke 4 in which Yeshua attends a synagogue, participates in its service, and reads the Haftarah portion (the Scripture reading from the Prophets) of the day. Much of the traditional synagogue service was already intact during Yeshua's time, as the Dead Sea Scrolls confirm. Fragments of scrolls of both daily and festival prayers dating to the Hasmonean period (first to second century B.C.E.), from the fourth cave at Qumran, show striking parallels to the traditional prayers in content, structure, and texts. Since the prayers in these scrolls exhibit nothing sectarian - unlike the other documents, which contain specific Qumran terminology and ideas - these prayers were part of the broader Jewish community. These findings lend support to the tradition that the men of the Great Assembly, reaching back approximately to 'Ezra's time, established the basic structure of the synagogue service followed to this day.

The synagogue, its service, and the cycle of readings are all "traditional" institutions, in which Yeshua approvingly participated, and His followers shared the same attachment to these traditional institutions. For example, there is strong evidence to suggest that the Gospels are structured as a commentary on the cycle of Jewish lexical and holiday readings. The Gospels also indicate Yeshua's use of prayers and blessings from the SIDDUR (prayer book), another product of the traditions. The Lord's Prayer of Matthew 6 reflects the third, fifth, sixth, and ninth benedictions of the Amidah (the central prayer of the synagogue service). In Luke 22:19 and following, Yeshua utilizes the traditional blessings over the bread.

Yeshua was Jewish, in every sense of the word. Broken Road Ministries acknowledges this. We all show complete reverence for where Yeshua confronted the ORAL LAWS of Judaism. Let us never forget the lesson which was learned. Many of the same practices (false practices of the Judaism sects) remain today, which were prevalent during Yeshua's time. Therefore, Broken Road Ministries avoids using the term "Messianic Judaism," as it creates confusion. We prefer to use the term "Messianic Movement."

Does the Messianic Movement keep Kosher?

Absolutely. We keep biblical "Kosher" for several reasons, the primary one being that YHWH has commanded us to do so. Despite the rejection of Elohim's commandments by other religions that claim to believe in the Bible, YHWH has never changed His policy regarding which animals He made for us to eat and which ones He made for other purposes.

Clean vs. Unclean

Long before Mosheh and the written law, YHWH distinguished His animals as being "TAHOR" (proper/clean) and "TAMEI" (improper/unclean). This distinction can be seen in His command for Noah to build the ark and take with him seven of every clean animal and two of every unclean (Genesis 7:2).

The familiar term "Kosher" is derived from the Hebrew word "KASHER" meaning, "to be right, correct, proper."

Didn't Yeshua do away with Elohim's commandments and make all food clean?

First of all, that obviously would make Elohim a liar since He specifically said that He does not change (Malachi 3:6) and that His word is forever settled in heaven (Psalm 119:89). Secondly, although proponents for eating unclean animals so often try to use (Mark 7:1-23, Matthew 15:1-20) to support their hope that Yeshua did away with

Elohim's commandments, the entire incident with Yeshua and the Pharisees revolved around the issue of "washing hands" - not the eating of unclean animals. The religious leaders were offended that Yeshua and His talmidim failed to obey their "TAKANOT" (man-made rules) regarding handwashing before eating. The subject of violating YHWH's "food laws" was never once mentioned.

What about Kefa's (Peter) vision of the sheet coming down from heaven with unclean animals and Elohim commanding him to eat?

Turn to Acts 10:9-28. As you read it for yourself, please notice two things:

(1) Kefa had never eaten unclean animals in his life (verse 10:14), so if Yeshua had done away with Elohim's commandments regarding the "food laws" then Kefa clearly disobeyed Messiah by not eating pigs, dogs, and rats.

(2) The meaning of the vision was revealed in (verse 10:28) and had nothing to do with actually eating unclean animals, but rather the acceptance by the Jewish believers of the Gentile converts coming into the faith.

Because of the pagan worship, perverted sexual practices and unclean eating practices of Gentiles (then and today), Jews understandably viewed ALL Gentiles as "unclean." To make His point clear to a Torah-observant Jew such as Kefa, YHWH used unclean animals in a vision to represent Gentiles (divine sarcasm). Elohim was preparing Kefa to receive the first Renewed Covenant Gentile converts into the faith who were no longer to be viewed as spiritually unclean.

Nowhere in this story did YHWH change His commandments regarding unclean "food," and nowhere in the Renewed Covenant Scriptures did Elohim's people ever begin eating unclean animals.

Does the Messianic Movement observe Sabbath?

Absolutely. The first-century synagogue service is briefly described in Luke 4:16-21. Notice the reading from the Torah and from the Haftarah (a selection from the Prophets). When Yeshua turned to Isaiah 61, a messianic section, He read from the Haftarah portion. The last reader in the service was customarily given the honor of expounding on the reading with a sermon, which was why Yeshua spoke on fulfilling the words of the prophet Isaiah.

Yeshua made it His habit to worship at the weekly Shabbat service. What else would He do? He was born a Jew and lived a life consistent with much of traditional Judaism of His day. Likewise, the first Jewish disciples continued in the traditional forms of synagogue worship (see Acts 13:14 and 18:4). This does not imply that Yeshua agreed with every detail of every rabbinic teaching of Sabbath observance. Indeed, He tried to correct imbalances in rabbinic perspective by reminding the people that "Shabbat was made for mankind, not mankind for Shabbat" (Mark 2:27). Yeshua challenged the people of His day to remain biblically balanced, to enter into the true rest of Elohim's Spirit.

Yeshua affirmed the keeping of Shabbat.

He desired that His people get past the traditions that obscured the true meaning of Shabbat. He wanted them to experience the blessing of rest, the remembrance of the Creation, the recollection of the covenant Elohim had made with Israel, and the realization that Shabbat was a picture of eternity - one that humanity could enjoy in the present age. Nowhere did Yeshua teach that Shabbat could be broken. In fact, He always went to the synagogue on Shabbat. In the entire Renewed Testament, there is not one reference to the believers (nearly all Jewish) violating Shabbat. Yeshua loved the Shabbat. On His missionary journeys, the Emissary Sha' ul (Apostle Paul) always went to the synagogue on this holy day - not for evangelism, but for worship. The Renewed Testament repeatedly states that He went "as His custom was." He was an observant Jew. Other Apostles, too, worshipped on Shabbat. Nowhere does the Renewed Testament teach against obtaining the blessing of Shabbat.

What is replacement theology?

The Christian religion practices Replacement Theology which comes fashioned in a variety of doctrinal teachings, one of those teachings is "The Rapture.'

Replacement Theology basically teaches that the church replaced Israel and that Elohim is not going to keep His promise to restore Israel. Hence, in the doctrine of the rapture; Elohim is not restoring Israel. Part of this doctrine includes the teaching that The Holy Spirit will be going somewhere. He won't be here, while those left behind must suffer through the Great Tribulation without Him. Meanwhile, there is no mention of the Holy Spirit ever leaving earth at all. Furthermore, though proponents of this view insist that "Elohim won't put us through" the Great Tribulation the Scriptures tell a much different story (Ezekiel 20:35-36 - 1 Corinthians 10:11-12).

In Replacement Theology, the Israel that we read about in the "Old" Testament was "physical" Israel while the "church" is "spiritual" Israel. The word "church" is a man-made word generally associated with the Catholic and Christian religions. In that context, it is typically meant to describe the corporate body of faith. It is used in most modern English Bibles as a translation for the Greek word EKKLESIA. The word "church" drives from pagan origins and its misuse is part of the problem associated with Replacement Theology, which teaches the "church" has replaced Israel, and that Elohim is not going to restore Israel like He has promised. Hence, the theory of The Rapture. It is essentially suggesting that when Elohim makes a Covenant, He no longer keeps the former ones.

Moreover, it reduces Elohim to the thinking power of a mortal man by insinuating that He must change His mind in order to get things right. Rather, we know that He is eternal and so is everything He does. The plan was right from the beginning.

Sinners Prayer

You shall receive power when the Holy Spirit has come upon you; and you shall be witnesses to Me in Jerusalem, and in all Judea and Samaria, and to the end of the earth. -Acts 1:8 (NKJV)

How do we receive the Holy Spirit?

If ye then, being evil, know how to give good gifts unto your children: how much more shall your heavenly Father give the Holy Spirit to them that ask him? -Luke 11:13 (KJV)

I often say the following prayer, as an exercise in obedience. Every day we must come to the foot of the cross and negotiate the terms of a full surrender.

Adon Yeshua, my heart is restless, and I need you. I am filled with a deep sorrow for my sins. I ask for Your forgiveness. I believe You came and died for my sins, and that You rose again on the third day. By grace through faith, I receive You as my Adon and Savior and Master. Thank you Adon Yeshua for giving me the gift of eternal life. Thank you Adon Yeshua for the promise of an abundant life. Please continue to change me from the inside out. Amen.

Elohim will meet you where you're at, but He won't let you stay there forever.

And by this we know that we have come to know Him, if we keep His commandments. Whoever says, "I know Him" but does not keep His commandments is a liar, and the truth is not in him, but whoever keeps His word, in him truly the love of Elohim is perfected. By this we may know that we are in him: whoever says he abides in Him ought to walk in the same way in which He walked. -1 John 2:3-6 (ESV)

You have to be in fellowship with Elohim if you want Him to answer your prayers. How do you get to know Elohim better? Read the bible. Yeshua is in the word in the flesh. Ask Him to speak to you through the word.

Messianic Shabbat service Guide

1) Opening Prayer
2) Kindling of the lights
3) Opening Blessing
4) Put on Tallits
5) Shema (facing east toward Jerusalem)
6) Blowing of the Shofar and Blessing of the Shofar
7) Worship music
8) S'udat Ha'adon
9) Torah portion
10) Prayer for Welcoming the Sabbath
11) Aaronic Blessing

- At times the leaders of the service may want to substitute certain prayers/blessings. It is OK to have variation. Keep in mind that there should never be mindless repetition; the Messiah warned rote words would not be heard. So always keep it fresh, and make sure (first and foremost) that the main focus of the service is TEACHING THE TORAH. Tradition should not quench the Ruach Ha'Kodesh (Holy Spirit).

Did Yeshua
abolish 'The Law'?

For a very long time (46 years) I was under the impression that 1) Christianity was not a religion, and as a Christian I would somehow be able to dodge the doctrines of men. 2) My belief was that we were called Christians because we did as Christ did. 3) And it was my belief that if a man wanted to confess the death and resurrection of the Messiah, Christianity was the only option. But I could not have been more wrong, on all these points.

Let's address each one of these points. 1) That Christianity is not a religion.
That is in fact, wrong. Christianity was the official state religion of the Roman Empire. Notice how I used the word: religion. Emperor Constantine made Christianity the official state religion through the Council of Nicaea in 325 C.E. He, himself was a sun worshipper of the goddess mithras. Christianity was not created by the Messiah.

The Roman Empire outlawed the Sabbath and anyone caught observing it was persecuted. They decreed there would be a day called "Rest Day," every Sunday; that it would not be Friday evening to Saturday evening as Yeshua observed it. They changed the Holy Days (commanded in Lev. 23) to their pagan holidays: Christmas and Easter. Paul who confessed the Torah (Acts 24:14, Acts 25:8) had warned that worship of the Messiah would be changed, that wolves would creep in.

"For I know this, that after my departure savage wolves shall come in among you, not sparing the flock. - Acts 20:29

Peter warned about Paul's writings being distorted:
..as also in all this (Paul's) letters, speaking in them of these things, in which are some things hard to understand, which the untaught and unstable distort, as they do also the rest of the Scriptures (Torah and the Prophets), to their own destruction. - 2 Peter 3:16

Now - as part of the Messianic Movement - I am committed to restoring worship of the Messiah back to how Yeshua and the disciples lived.

2) My belief was that Christians do as the Messiah did. But let's consider this for a moment. Yeshua was the living Torah (Christian Bibles refer to it as the Law. But how or why would Yeshua abolish Himself). He followed the Lunar Calendar (Creator's Calendar) not the Roman Solar Calendar. Yeshua observed Sabbath and the Appointed Times rather than Christmas and Easter. The Messiah did many things that Christians believe they do not have to do. Therefore, the confession: "We do as He did," did not seem to apply to me anymore.

"Do not think that I came to destroy the Torah or thc Prophets. I did not come to destroy but to fulfill. For assuredly, I say to you, till heaven and earth pass away, one jot or one tittle will by no means pass from the Torah till all are fulfilled. Whoever therefore breaks one of the least of these commandments, and teaches men so, shall be called least in the kingdom of heaven but whoever does and teaches them, he shall be called great in the kingdom of heaven."
- Matthew 5:17-19

This passage of Scripture does not create confusion, it provides clarity; for those who are able to receive what it is saying. The Greek word translated as "fulfill" is PLEROSAI which means: to fill up, to fully preach, to make full, to make complete. It does not mean: to destroy, dissolve or demolish which is KATALOOSAI in the Greek.

Fulfill (PLEROSAI) and Destroy (KATALOOSAI) are being juxtaposed as opposites, in this Scripture. So, if it's not one, it's the other. Fulfill cannot mean "to fully preach" and "to destroy" at the same time. But essentially, that is what Christianity is claiming; they are taking both POLAR OPPOSITE meanings of the Scripture and combining them.

So, what does FULFILL mean here? Well, Yeshua told us what it means: whoever does AND teaches them.

Isn't that what Yeshua did? He did AND taught the Torah. This is what it means to fulfill it. And He is telling you to do as He did. Do you claim to do as He did?

What did He mean when He said: till the heavens and earth pass away? Clearly the heavens and earth have not yet passed away.

And I saw a renewed heavens and a renewed earth, for the former heavens and the former earth had passed away, and the sea is no more. - Revelation 21:1

John's vision here is what will be after the thousand-year reign. John saw the new heavens and new earth (8th day). What Yeshua is saying is that we are to observe The Torah until the Bride (New Jerusalem) is presented to our Eternal King Yeshua, on the 8th day (Eternal dimension). Remember the day that Israel said, "I do," we vowed to follow the Torah (wedding contract).

We have been scattered throughout the world into exile, due to our disobedience.

And all the people answered together and said, "All that YHWH has spoken we shall do." So, Moses brought back the words of the people to YHWH. - Exodus 19:8

This day is called Shavuot. This is the day that Israel agreed to their marriage vows (the wedding contract known as the Torah). Pentecost (The day we received the Holy Spirit) was on the anniversary of Shavuot. We agreed to live by the Torah on the same day of the year that we received The Holy Spirit. This is rather significant, for many reasons. But still, many are unable to receive this. And in fact, the word "Lawlessness" comes from the Greek word ANOMIA, which means "without the instructions of the Torah."

So which Scripture has resolved the issue for you? It should be what Yeshua said.

For if you believed Moses, you would believe Me, for he wrote about Me. But if you do not believe his writings, How are you going to believe MY WORDS? - John 5:46-47
3) If a person wants to confess the death and resurrection of the Messiah, Christianity is their only option. That is wrong. The Messianic Movement is growing at a fast rate. These are people who want the truth at any cost. They want worship to be restored to what Yeshua and the disciples were doing without the changes which were made by the Roman Empire.

And Yeshua answering, said to them, Elijah is indeed coming first, and shall restore all. - Matthew 17:11

The Messianic Movement involves the Spirit of Elijah restoring worship of the Messiah to how it was before the Roman Empire corrupted it. It's the voice crying out in the wilderness, to prepare the world for the coming of the Messiah; like it did the first time.

"See, I am sending you Elijah the prophet before the coming of the great and awesome day of YHWH. - Malachi 4:5

If everyone is doing as the Messiah did, there should be one movement; without multiple sects and denominations. Members of Yeshua's body are called to bear with one another in love, endeavoring to keep the unity of the Spirit in the bond of peace." (Ephesians 4:3).

Ruling with Yeshua for a thousand years

And it shall be in the latter days that the mountain of the House of YHWH is established on the top of the mountains and shall be exalted above the hills. And all nations shall flow to it. And many peoples shall come and say, "Come, and let us go up to the mountain of YHWH, to the House of the Elohim of Ya' aqob, and let him teach us His ways, and let us walk in His paths, FOR OUT OF TSIYON COMES FORTH THE TORAH, and the Word of YHWH from Yerushalayim." And He shall judge between the nations and shall reprove many peoples. And they shall beat their swords into ploughshares, and their spears into pruning hooks. Nation shall not lift up sword against nation, neither teach battle anymore. - Isaiah 2:2-4

Yeshua will teach the Torah from Mount Zion.

And it will come about in the last days that the mountain of the house of YHWH will be established as the chief of the mountains. It will be raised above the hills, and the peoples will stream to it. And many nations will come and say, "Come and let us go up to the mountain of YHWH and to the house of the Elohim of Jacob, that He may teach us about His ways and that we may walk in His paths. For from Zion will go forth the Torah, even the word of YHWH from Jerusalem. And He will judge between many peoples and render decisions for mighty, distant nations. Then they will hammer their swords into plowshares and their spears into pruning hooks. Nation will not lift up sword against nation, and never again will they train for war. - Micah 4:1-3

If you do not know the Torah, then you cannot help Yeshua rule by the Torah during the thousand-year reign.

Whoever, then breaks one of the least of these Commands, and teaches men so, shall be called least in the reign of the shamayim; but whoever does and teaches them, he shall be called great in the reign of the shamayim
. - Matthew 5:19

To be least in the kingdom means you will not be a ruler. You can still make it into the kingdom through the second resurrection (white throne judgment).

And I saw thrones, and they sat upon them, and judgment was given to them. And I saw the souls of those who had been beheaded because of the testimony of Yeshua and because of the word of Elohim, and those who had not worshiped the beast or his image and had not received the mark upon their forehead and upon their hand; and they came to life and reigned with Yeshua for a thousand years. The rest of the dead did not come to life until the thousand years were completed. This is the resurrection. Blessed and holy is the one who has a part in the first resurrection. Over these the second death has no power, but they will be priests of Elohim and of Yeshua and will reign with Him for a thousand years. - Revelation 20:4-6

Answer the Following Questions:

1. When and how was Christianity established as a religion?

_____
_____
_____
_____

2. Who outlawed the Sabbath, and what was it replaced with?

_____
_____
_____
_____

3. Read Daniel 7:24-25. What did the Roman Empire replace the Appointed Times (Leviticus 23) with? Explain how the Scripture in Daniel relates to this.

_____
_____
_____
_____

4. Some people say "they do as Yeshua" did. But after a close comparison, we find that there are certain things the Messiah did which they refuse to acknowledge. Give some examples of practices which the Messiah had partaken in, which are not followed today.

_____
_____
_____
_____

5. The English word "fulfill" comes from what Greek word? What does this Greek word mean?

_____
_____
_____
_____

6. The English word "destroy" comes from what Greek word? What does this Greek word mean?

_____
_____
_____
_____

7. Read Matthew 5:17-19. Taking into account the meaning of the Greek words above, what does it mean to "fulfill the Torah"?

_____
_____
_____
_____

8. Read Matthew 5:17-19. Read Revelation 21:1. Explain the meaning of "till the heavens and earth pass away."

_____

_____

_____

_____

9. What is the 8th day? What will happen on the 8th day?

_____

_____

_____

_____

10. The English word "lawlessness" comes from what Greek word? What does this Greek word mean?

_____

_____

_____

_____

11. What will the "Spirit of Elijah" do at the end of the age to make a way for the second coming of the Messiah?

_____

_____

_____

_____

12. Read Isaiah 2:2-4. Read Micah 4:1-3. What is similar about these two passages of Scripture, in regard to the Torah?

_____

_____

_____

_____

13. Read Revelation 20:4-6. What is the advantage of being part of the first resurrection?

_____

_____

_____

_____

14. Lawlessness means "without the Torah." Yeshua will rule by the Torah for a thousand years. Those who do not live by the Torah and teach others to not live by the Torah will be least in the kingdom. What then can we conclude about the first resurrection and those who know the Torah and teach the Torah?

_____

_____

_____

_____

Ethnicity won't save you

Yeshua wasn't white. We all know this. Yet there are some circles in which He is portrayed as having a milky white skin color. People born in the middle east do not look like that. Perhaps He was not as black as is portrayed in the cover of this book, but that is OK. The cover is making an important statement, mainly that: Ethnicity won't save you.

The Apostle Paul spent a great deal of energy preaching this very message. So much in fact; that his message was sometimes perceived as being anti-Torah, which in fact it wasn't. Paul confessed the Torah (what the Christians call the Law).

"And this I confess to you, that according to the Way which they call a sect, so I worship the Elohim of my fathers, believing all that has been written in the Torah and in the Prophets. - Acts 24:14

Back then there was no Renewed Testament (Christians call it the New Testament). Paul and the Apostles taught the Gospel from the Torah.

"while Paul said in his own defense, neither against the Torah of the Yahudim, nor against the Temple, nor against Ceasar did I commit any sin." - Acts 25:8

What Paul was communicating is that you are not guaranteed a place in the Kingdom simply because you are Jewish (ETHNICITY WON'T SAVE YOU). Anyone can be grafted in who 1) confesses the death and resurrection of the Messiah and 2) lives in obedience to the Torah (wedding contract) which is the constitution of the Kingdom.

Remember that when Israel left Egypt they were saved by the Blood of the Lamb (which Yeshua would later fulfill by being the Passover sacrifice) and therefore their first-born was spared by the angel of death. However, even after the parting of the Rea Sea they were still not spared in the wilderness due to their refusal to adhere to the Torah (wedding contract). IT IS BOTH: BLOOD OF MESSIAH AND TORAH. You cannot separate the BRIDE (ISRAEL) and the Wedding Contract.

You are only JEWISH if 1) You or your ancestry are from Judah (Southern Kingdom - 2 Tribes) or 2) you practice the religion JUDAISM (created by the Pharisees). And in neither of these instances are you guaranteed a place in the Kingdom. This is NOT a message of antisemitism, quite the opposite. It is false teachings which perpetuate antisemitism. And it is time that those wrongs be made right.

There is no such thing as MESSIANIC JUDAISM. The more accurate term is MESSIANIC MOVEMENT.

Judaism was created by the Pharisees, and they meditate on Talmudic Traditions or Kabbalistic mysticism. Yeshua was against making the Torah a burden by adding man-made traditions (Matthew 11:30 - Mark 7:4 - Galatians 1:14).

Written in the Talmud are the laws and traditions which constitute the oral Torah of Judaism. They are specifically known as the Takanot and Ma'asim. The word Takanot means "enactments" and refers to the laws enacted by the Pharisees. Ma'asim literally means "works or deeds" and refers to the precedents of the Rabbis that provide the source for Pharisaic rulings.
PAUL WAS NOT SPEAKING AGAINST THE TORAH. HE WAS SPEAKING AGAINST THE ORAL TORAH. Why? There is no ORAL TORAH. Moses wrote everything down.

So Moses came and told the people all the Words of YHWH and all the judgments. And all the people answered with one voice and said, All the words which YHWH has said we will do. And Moses wrote all the words of YHWH. - Exodus 24:3-4

Yeshua came to restore the Torah to it's rightful place and part of His ministry involved confronting the self-imposed authority of the Pharisees and their Oral Torah. Paul would never disrespect the Messiah and His sacrifice. Nor will we. Paul spoke so strongly against the Oral Torah that some misunderstood him as being against YHWH's Torah. Peter spoke about this kind of confusion.

as also in all his (Paul's) letters, speaking in them of these things, in which are some things hard to understand, which the untaught and unstable distort, as they do also the rest of the Scriptures (Torah and the Prophets), to their own destruction. - 2 Peter 3:16

Many claim they do AS THE MESSIAH DID, but they do not. If all of us were doing as He did, there would be no division or denominations. There would simply be ONE MOVEMENT.

Paul further teaches: "stand fast in one spirit, with one mind" and to be "of one accord and one mind." (Philippians 1:27 and 2:2).

The Torah instructs Israel to teach the Torah (or what Christians call the Law) to all people. The Torah serves as the Constitution to the Kingdom. It applies to ALL of YHWH's people. At times, the Scriptures refer to the WHOLE of YHWH's people as the mixed multitude (Exodus 12:37-38 - Genesis 17:5 - 32:12 - 48:16,19 - 2 Samuel 6:19 - 1 Kings 3:8).

Assemble the people, the men and the women and children and the alien who is in your town, in order that they may hear and learn and fear YHWH your Elohim and be careful to observe all the words of this Torah. - Deuteronomy 31:12

Did YHWH say to Moses, "Now Moses, separate out for Me two peoples. On my right hand place the physical descendants of Jacob, who will one day be called 'Jews.' To them I will give the Torah with Sabbath and festivals. And on the other hand, gather all the future "non-Jews" who will receive "grace" and two commandments: love Elohim and everyone else."? No.

It didn't happen that way. Instead, Elohim said through Moses for all people to be gathered, let the world hear this loud and clear.

When it came to Passover and the Feast of Unleavened Bread, when the Messiah would offer Himself as the Lamb of Elohim, Elohim instructed us to keep the Passover this way:

Seven days there shall be no leaven found in your houses, for whoever eats what is leavened, that person shall be cut off from the congregation of Israel, whether he is an alien or a native of the land. - Exodus 12:19

He also said that everyone, even the alien, is to be circumcised (in the heart) to eat the Passover.

In fact, Paul instructed the Corinthians to observe the Passover:

Your boasting is not good. Do you not know that a little leaven leavens the entire lump? Therefore, cleanse out the old leaven, so that you are a new lump, as you are unleavened. For also Mashiach our Pesah was offered for us.

So then let us observe the Festival, not with old leaven, nor with the leaven of evil and wickedness, but with the unleavened bread of sincerity and truth. - 1 Corinthians 5:6-8

Grace is a word found more times in the First (or Old) Testament than in the Renewed (or New Testament). When you confess with your mouth (Romans 10:9) you enter into a wedding contract. The same wedding contract given in Exodus 19:8. It involves our vow to the Covenant.

So, we come into a Covenant with Yeshua by grace through faith and cannot break that Covenant. It's like me being invited into your house and you ask me to come in by grace. You give me a place of honor in your home. You put me in your will, in your testament. Then I choose not to obey any of the commandments you establish in your house. I was a guest. By grace you asked me to stay. My obedience keeps me in the blessing. Grace allows you in the door, obedience keeps you in the blessing. At some point, all grace periods end.

Remember, that Israel was saved by the Blood of the Lamb (Yeshua's Blood) and their first born were spared by the angel of death. Later, Yeshua would fulfill Passover when He was the Passover sacrifice.

However, even after crossing the parted Red Sea many were not spared in the wilderness because of their refusal to adhere to the Torah. Clearly, it is both: CONFESSING THAT YESHUA DIED AND WAS RESURRECTED AND ADHERENCE TO THE TORAH. Israel is the Bride. You cannot separate the bride from the wedding contract.

At some point, the grace period will end. In fact, we will once again be subject to the Torah at the end of the age, as were our fathers.

"And I shall bring you out from the peoples and gather you out of the lands where you are scattered, with a mighty hand, and with an outstretched arm, and with wrath poured out.

And I shall bring you into the wilderness of the peoples and shall enter into judgment with you face to face there.

As I entered into judgment with your fathers in the wilderness of the land of Egypt, so I shall enter into judgment with you," declares the Adon YHWH. - Ezekiel 20:34-36

It is easy to see why the satan would want the world not to observe the Torah at the end of the age. Clearly, he does not want YHWH's people to repent. The devil would rather convince us that the natural disasters coming upon the world are due to global warming. If he can do this, we will simply address the effects of YHWH's judgments as being a problem with carbon emissions and greenhouse gases, rather than change our ways.

Interestingly, Paul also warns us; that we will once again need to adhere to the Torah as did our fathers when they were in the wilderness. He warns us not to make the same mistakes they did.

For I do not want you to be ignorant, brothers, that all our fathers were under the cloud, and all passed through the sea, and all passed through the sea, and all were immersed into Moses in the cloud and in the sea, and all ate the same spiritual food, and all drank the same spiritual drink. For they drank of that spiritual Rock that followed, and the Rock was Mashiach.

However, with most of them Elohim was not well pleased, for they were laid low in the wilderness.

And these became examples for us, so that we should not lust after evil, as those indeed lusted. And do not become idolaters as some of them, as it has been written, "The people sat down to eat and to drink, and stood up to play."

Neither should we commit whoring, as some of them did, and in one day twenty-three thousand fell, neither let us try Mashiach, as some of them also tried, and were destroyed by serpents, neither grumble, as some of them grumbled, and were destroyed by the destroyer.

And all these came upon them as examples, and they written as a warning to us, on whom the ends of the ages have come so that he who thinks he stands, let him take heed lest he fall.
- 1 Corinthians 10:1-12

Clearly, Paul (led by the Holy Spirit) is telling us that we will once again be UNDER THE CLOUD in the wilderness - at the end of the age - just like our fathers. There will be another exodus. Isaiah, writing long after the first exodus; also tells us we will be under the cloud.

then YHWH shall create above every dwelling place of Mount Zion, and above her assemblies, a cloud and smoke by day and the shining of a flaming fire by night, for over all the esteem shall be a covering, and a booth for shade in the daytime from the heat, for a place of refuge, and for a shelter from storm and rain.
- Isaiah 4:5-6

Remember, that the past will repeat itself. If you want to know what happens at the end, go back to beginning.

Two witnesses, Judgments, Exodus.

Two witnesses, (instead of Moses and Aaron there will be two different witnesses), Judgments (Instead of ten judgments on Egypt there will be 7 seals - 3 judgments each or 21 total on the whole world), and an Exodus (instead of an exodus out of Egypt it will be an exodus from all over the world; all those who have been grafted into the Kingdom).

Ezekiel was told to join the two sticks (Ezekiel 37:16). The first stick (first exodus) happened in 1948. That was the Two Tribes from Judah. The next stick (next exodus) is Ephraim or Israel. the other ten tribes (Those who have been grafted-in - Roman 11:15-25).

Remember this, and show yourselves men. Turn it back, you transgressors. Remember the former of long ago, for I am El, and there is no else - Elohim, and there is no one like Me, declaring the end from the beginning, and from of old that which has not been done, saying, 'My counsel stands, and all My delight I do.' - Isaiah 46:8-10

Thus said YHWH, Sovereign of Yisrael, and his Redeemer, YHWH of Hosts, 'I am the First and I am the Last, besides Me there is no Elohim. - Isaiah 44:6

And behold,some are last who will be first, and some are first who will be last. - Luke 13:30

"I am the 'Aleph' and the 'Tau', the Beginning and the End, the First and the Last. - Revelation 22:13

If you want to know what happens at the end, go back to beginning. It's all going to repeat itself. There is nothing new under the sun.

What has been is what will be, and what has been done is what will be done, and there is nothing new under the sun - Ecclesiastes 1:9

Answer the Following Questions:

1. Write out Acts 24:14 below. Write out Acts 25:8 below. According to these Scriptures, did Paul confess to follow the Torah?

_____
_____
_____
_____
_____
_____
_____
_____
_____

2. Before Israel left Egypt (and the bond of slavery) were they saved by the Blood of Yeshua. If so, explain how.

_____
_____
_____
_____

3. What is the definition of "Jewish"? If you are Jewish are you guaranteed a place in the Kingdom?

_____
_____
_____
_____

4. The term "MESSIANIC MOVEMENT" is a more accurate term than "MESSIANIC JUDAISM." Explain why the term "MESSIANIC JUDAISM" can be misconstrued and lead some astray in regard to the goal of our imitating the Messiah.

_____
_____
_____
_____
_____
_____
_____

5. What is the "ORAL TORAH" of Judaism? What constitutes the man-made laws of Judaism?

_____
_____
_____
_____
_____
_____
_____
_____

6. Read Exodus 24:3-4. Read 2 Peter 3:16. Is there an ORAL TORAH? Or did Moses write everything down? How have people twisted the Torah and the Prophets to their own destruction?

_____
_____
_____
_____
_____
_____

7. Read Deuteronomy 31:12. Read Exodus 12:19. What is the constitution of the Kingdom? Is anyone excluded from it? Why or why not?

_____
_____
_____
_____
_____
_____
_____

8. Read Romans 10:9. Read Exodus 19:8. When you confess with your mouth that Yeshua is the Messiah, and that He died and rose again; what are you agreeing to? What is the vow you have made?

_____
_____
_____
_____

9. Read Ezekiel 20:34-36. Read Isaiah 4:5-6. What will repeat itself at the end of age? According to this Scripture, what will happen at the end of the grace period?

_____

_____

_____

_____

_____

10. Read Ezekiel 37:16-22. What are the two sticks that Ezekiel was asked to join together into one stick? What does each stick represent?

_____

_____

_____

_____

_____

_____

11. Was the exodus done in 1948, or is there still more come? Explain.

_____

_____

_____

_____

613 Mitzvot
Or
Laws in the Torah

Somehow a Jewish tradition has been passed down through history that leads many to believe there are 613 Mitzvot or Laws in the Torah that are written and meant to be kept. This number is used by some to attempt to prove that we cannot keep all the laws and thus highlight the need for forgiveness of Ha' Mashiach, while some even claim that they are a burden!

While it is most definitely true that we Do need redemption through Yeshua, as we have all fallen short of the perfection of YHWH (sometimes grace must pick us up and carry us) the simple truth is, that even Yeshua did not keep all these so-called 613 laws. Why?

Because the commands given in the Torah are specified to whom they pertain.
A large portion of the laws are for the Kohenim, some just for men, some just for women, some for animals or the owners of animals, etc.

Approximately 30% of the laws are specifically for the Kohenim, with about 30% divided into percentages for the Kohen ha'gadol, judges, sovereigns, servants, etc. and the remaining 41% actually apply to everyone who considers themselves part of Yisra'el regardless of position or condition.

It is the constitution of the kingdom for all of Elohim's people; with respect to whom it applies.

Hanukkah - Festival of Lights

"They kept 8 festal days with rejoicing in the manner of SUKKOT, remembering how not long before at the time of the Feast of Tabernacles they had been living in the mountains and caves like wild animals. Then carrying branches, leafy boughs and palms, they offered hymns to Him (YHWH) who had brought the cleansing of His own holy place to a happy outcome. They also decreed by a public proclamation, ratified by vote, that the whole Jewish nation should celebrate these same days every year."
- 2 Maccabees 10:1-9

Hanukkah, also known as the Feast of Dedication or the Festival of Lights, is a holiday commemorating the rededication of the second Temple. It is a celebration of faith and commitment to Elohim's Word.

Hanukkah commemorates the story in Israel's history of a small group of Jewish believers who, by Elohim's strength, successfully defeated the forces of evil in their time. They took back the Holy Temple in Jerusalem from pagan idol worshipers. The perversion of the Greek Gentile religion (the basis for the later Roman religion) and its abomination of desolation were irradicated from the Temple so it could be rededicated to the ONE true Elohim of Israel (not multiple golds like that of pagan religions. We remember that the Messiah Himself took back our personal "temples" from the enemy and rededicated us to Elohim. Therefore, we see Hanukkah as a rededication of the altar of our hearts.

Interestingly enough, the only reference to Hanukkah in the Scriptures is found in the Renewed Testament:

At the time the Feast of Dedication took place at Jerusalem. It was winter, and Yeshua was walking in the temple, in the colonnade of Solomon - John 10:22-23

They celebrated it for eight days with rejoicing, in the manner of the festival of booths, remembering how not long before, during the festival of booths, they had been wandering in the mountains and caves like wild animals. Therefore, carrying ivy-wreathed wands and beautiful branches and also fronds of palm, they offered hymns of thanksgiving to him who had given success to the purifying of his own holy place. They decreed by public edict, ratified by vote, that the whole nation of the Jews should observe these days every year -2 Maccabees 10:6-8

HANUKKAH BLESSING

The MENORAH (candleholder) used Hanukkah is called a "HANUKIAH" pronounced "HA-NOO-KEEYA" and has a total of (9) candleholders instead of the standard (7) candles on a traditional MENORAH. Eight candles represent the 8-days of Hanukkah with the ninth candle (the middle one) called SHAMMASH (Servant). This servant candle is used to light the other candles as Hanukkah candles are only meant to be looked upon and not used kindle other fires (i.e., candles, fireplaces, stoves, etc). One candle (light) is kindled for each of the eight nights of Hanukkah beginning with the candle on the right side, always moving to the left.

BEFORE LIGHTING THE CANDLES

Blessed are You, YHWH our Elohim, King of the Universe Who have sanctified us with Your Spirit and enabled us to light these Hanukkah lights, Who performed miracles for our forefathers in those days, at this time, and have given us life, sustained us, and enabled us to reach this season.

BA-ROOKH A-TA YHWH, ME-LEKH HA-O-LAHM KEED-SHANOO BUH-ROO-KHA-KHA, V'HEE-GEE-ANOO LUH-HAD-LEEK NAYR SHEL KHA-NOO-KA.

SHUH-ASAH NEE-SEEM LA-AVO-TAY-NOO BAYA-MEEM HA-HAYM BEEZ-MAN HA-ZEH, OO-SHUH-HEKH-YANOO, VUH-KEEM-ANOO VUH-HEE-GEE-ANOO LAZMAN HA-ZEH.

AFTER LIGHTING THE CANDLES

We kindle the lights to commemorate the saving acts, miracles, and wonders YHWH our Elohim performed for our forefathers in those days, at this time.

Throughout the 8 days of Hanukkah, these lights are sacred to us. As we behold them, we give thanks and to YHWH our Father for His delivering power and to commemorate the season of conception of His only begotten Son, our Lord and Rabbi Yeshua the Messiah.

Hanukkah - Historical Background

2 Chronicles 36:23

To fully understand this holy day, one must go back to a tumultuous time in the history of Israel: the Hellenistic period around 167 B.C.E. As was so often the case, the Jewish people were living under the oppression of a foreign power. A few generations earlier, the Greeks had come to world power under the remarkable leadership of Alexander the Great. With the ascension of this kingdom, Alexander seemed to have unified the ancient world into one common government and culture, which is known as Hellenism.

But after Alexander's untimely death, there was a political scramble among four of his generals, resulting in the division of the Hellenistic empire. The Ptolemies took control of the south, which included Egypt, and the Seleucids took charge of the northern area around Syria. This left Judea caught in the middle of a tug-of-war. Eventually, under the leadership of Antiochus IV, the Seleucid/Syrians gained power and sought control of the new provinces. Seeking to unify his holdings, Antiochus enforced a policy of assimilation into the prevailing Hellenistic culture, requiring total submission to the Greek way of life.

The Greeks thought that to be truly effective, this assimilation must apply to all aspects of life, including language, the arts, and even religion. Everything was to conform to the "superior" Greek way of life and values. This did not present a major problem for many people under the Seleucids. Indeed, the Greeks were highly respected for their culture. Even many Jews in Judea had adopted the Hellenistic way and openly advocated adherence to it. However, there were a significant number of traditional Jews who were appalled at the changes in their society. Antiochus and the Seleucids continued growing more hostile toward these stubborn Jews who did not convert to Hellenism and steps were taken to enforce their policy. An ultimatum was given: either the Jewish community must give up its distinctive customs (Shabbat, kosher laws, circumcision, and so on) or die. To prove his point, Antiochus marched his troops in Yerushalayim and desecrated the holy Temple. The altars, the utensils, even the golden menorah were all torn down or defiled.

But that was just the beginning. Antiochus also ordered that a pig be sacrificed on the Jews' holy altar, and he erected an image of the greek Elohim Zeus (who, oddly enough, looked like Antiochus) as the new point of worship in the Temple. Antiochus insisted on being called Epiphanes ("Elohim manifest"), which would repulse any religious Jew. The Jewish community soon used a play on words, calling him "Epimanes," which means "crazy man."

The murmurings of revolt were heard in Judea, finally erupting in a small village called

Modi' in after Syrian troops entered the town to enforce their assimilation policy. The soldiers planned to erect a temporary altar to the false gods and force the populace to participate in their religious ceremony - the highlight of which was eating the flesh of the swine. Living in the village was an old, godly priest named Mattathias and his five sons. When the Seleucid soldiers chose him to lead the pagan ceremony, Mattathias and his sons reacted with holy indignation. They killed the soldiers and started a revolt against the oppressors. one of the sons, Y' hudah, rose to leadership and was nicknamed Maccabee, which means "the Hammer." Overwhelmingly outnumbered and undersupplied, the armies of the Maccabees turned to more creative devices. Relying on their knowledge of the hill country and employing guerrilla warfare, the Jewish forces met with surprising success. Spurred on by their firm conviction that the Elohim of Israel was true and faithful, the Maccabees proved that the impossible could happen. In the Hebrew month of Kislev (November/December) they drove out the Syrians and recaptured the Temple.

Now they faced the daunting task of restoring to the Temple the true worship of Elohim. As the Temple compound was in shambles, desecrated by the idolatry of the Syrians, the Maccabees and their followers quickly cleansed the altars and restored the holy furnishings.

Of particular importance to them was the broken menorah, symbolizing the light of Elohim. They restored it attempted to light it, but there was a problem. Jewish tradition recounts that as they searched for some specially prepared oil, they found only enough to burn for one day. The priests knew it would take at least eight days for new oil to be produced. What to do? They decided it was better to light the menorah anyway, at least the light of Elohim would shine forth immediately. To their amazement, the oil burned not only for one day, but for eight days until additional oil was available! The Temple was restored and rededicated to the glory of the Elohim of Israel and an eight-day festival was established called Hanukkah (Dedication). Every year, starting on the twenty-fifth of Kislev, the Jewish community recalls the twofold miracle: the miracle of the oil, as well as the miraculous military victory.

Traditional Jewish Observance

Hanukkah focuses on the HANUKKIYAH, the nine-branched menorah, or candleholder. Eight branches are reminder of the eight-day miracle of oil. A candle is lit the first day of Hanukkah, with an additional candle lit each subsequent day. The candle in the ninth branch (the center) is used to light the other candles. It is the SHAMASH (servant). The Menorah is lit after dark, usually in connection with a festive meal. After the blessings are said, it is traditional to sing holiday songs. Then it's time to enjoy the meal with its traditional foods. Because of the miracle of the oil, it is customary to eat foods cooked in oil, such as LATKES (potato pancakes) and SUFGANIYOT (Israeli jelly doughnuts). They may not be thebest for our diets, but they are a delicious way to remember the miracle of Elohim!

Another reminder of the miracle of this holy day is the game of DREYDELS. These wooden or plastic tops have different Hebrew letters on each of their four sides: Nun, Gimel, Hey, and Shin standing for the phrase NES GADAL HAYAH SHAM ("A Great Miracle Happened There"). More recently, the custom of giving gifts has found its way into the celebration of this joyous festival. Many families give real money (GELT) to children, perhaps twenty-five cents for each year of their age. Their is nothing wrong with these traditions. They are a Jewish adaptation in response to the Christmas gift-giving custom at the same time of the year.

Passover Haggadah

BARUKH HABA! "Welcome!"

Tonight, we celebrate the Feast of Passover (PESACH in Hebrew). It is the first of eight commanded festivals of our Elohim - YHWH. These are not "Jewish" festivals as they are often incorrectly referred to, but our Father Himself called them "His feasts (Leviticus 23:2), therefore, whether we were raised Jewish or we became Jewish through conversion of being grafted in - we are all commanded to keep them as His New Covenant children of the Olive Tree of Israel.

This day shall be to you a memorial and you shall keep it as a feast to YHWH throughout your generations. You shall keep it as a feast by an ordinance forever. - Exodus 12:14

As believers in the Jewish Messiah, (hence the term "Messianic"), we strive to follow the example set by YHWH's Son - Yeshua. Both He and His disciples (TALMIDIM) observed these feasts, as also did the early Renewed Covenant believers long after YESHUA's resurrection and return to His Father in Heaven.

Each of the eight festivals symbolically represent YESHUA in Elohim's plan of salvation with Passover as the starting point. The telling (HAGGADAH) of the Exodus story commemorates the deliverance of Israel from Egypt and foreshadows our redemption from sin and death by the sacrifice of the Lamb of

Elohim whose blood has been applied to the doorposts of our hearts.

So significant is this Passover feast that YESHUA instituted the Renewed Covenant (BRIT HADASHAH) during the very same Seder meal that we are celebrating tonight. The Hebrew term "SEDER" means "order" and refers to the specific instructions YHWH gave to His people regarding the keeping of Passover. We can clearly see this principle in the teaching of the emissary Shaul (Paul) who instructed us in (1 Corinthians 14:40) to,

"Let all things be done decently and in order (seder)."

Passover begins just before sunset on AVIV 14th and concludes a few hours later on AVIV 15th, ushering in the second feast of YHWH - the Feast of Unleavened Bread (HAG HA' MATZAH).

The SEDER Meal

The Seder meal is planned many days (sometimes weeks) prior to Passover with preparations and cooking beginning many hours beforehand. The traditional Seder ceremony lasts well over two hours to allow for all the readings and explanations to take place. Halfway through the ceremony the meal is eaten, music is played and everyone enjoys fellowship with family and friends.

Our services are always much shorter due to our time constraints, but we endeavor to maintain the symbolisms and traditions our ancestors have kept over the millennia - based on the resources we have available to us.

Throughout the ceremony, readings in both Hebrew and English will be done by various brethren. In many places, ALL of us will read aloud together. The Messianic Movement is more than just a faith, it is a community of believers that do "As Yeshua did."

The food items set before you and the other articles on the tables will be explained throughout the ceremony. If you have celebrated a Seder with us before . . . welcome back! If this is your first Seder, we hope you enjoy it.

Over the centuries, the tradition of using four cups of wine at specific times in the ceremony was initiated long before Yeshua was born in the town of Bethlehem (BEYT - LEKHEM). The symbolism of these four cups - as with everything in the TANAKH (Bible) - all center around YHWH's plan of salvation through His Son Yeshua:

Cup #1 - Cup of Sanctification
Cup #2 - Cup of Judgment
Cup #3 - Cup of Redemption
Cup #4 - Cup of Acceptance

B' DEKAT HAMETZ (The Search for Leaven)

Passover begins the weeklong period of abstaining from all foods made with leaven (yeast). Why would YHWH command such a thing? (Exodus 12:18-20) It is not that leaven itself is bad, but during this holy period of Passover and Unleavened Bread, the leaven comes to symbolize that which Yeshua died for our sins. The purpose of leaven is to cause a lump of dough to rise. When sin is allowed to cultivate in our lives, we become full of ourselves, proud, arrogant, and puffed up.

READER

"Do you not know that a little leaven, leavens the whole lump? Therefore remove the old leaven so that you may be a new lump, since truly you are without leaven. For Messiah, our Passover, was sacrificed for us, therefore let us keep the Feast. Not with old leaven, nor the leaven of malice and wickedness, but with the unleavened bread of sincerity and truth." - 1 Corinthians 5:6-8

The Jewish tradition of removing HAMETZ (leaven) from the home was a family affair and as always involved the children. A search is made with a candle to see into the dark areas and a feather was used to reach the hidden corners of cupboards and cabinets. The HAMETZ was then swept onto a wooden spoon, wrapped in a cloth or paper bag and carried outside. A celebration was made as the HAMETZ was burned for all to see - a statement to the world that, "This house is clean!"

CANDLE = The Word of Elohim (Torah) revealing the sin in our lives.
FEATHER = YHWH's Spirit that softly guides us to the tree.
SPOON = The piece of wood used to remove our sins.
FIRE = YHWH Himself is a consuming fire! (Hebrews 12:29)

LEADER

At this point in our ceremony, I must ask that each of you check your shirt and pants pockets for any leaven items you may have unknowingly brought in tonight. Cookies, bread and crackers are not permitted while we celebrate the Seder meal.

Lighting of the Seder Candles

For every Shabbat and Feast of YHWH, the honor of lighting the candles is given to the woman of the house. The eldest woman and the youngest girl will light the candles, encircling them three times with their hands as to draw in the warmth of the flames and then cover their eyes. After they say the blessing, they remove their hands from their eyes and the first thing they behold is the candle's light symbolizing the glory of YHWH our Elohim.

Since we have no woman among us to do this honor, let us say the blessing together:

**Blessed are You, YHWH our Elohim,
King of the universe,
Who has sanctified us by Your Spirit
and given us Yeshua our Messiah
Who commanded us to be the
light of the world. Amen**

Passover Reading (Exodus 12:1-14)

READER #1 YHWH spoke to Moses and Aaron in the land of Egypt and said, "This month shall be your beginning of months. It shall be the first month of the year to you. Speak to the whole community of Israel and tell them that on the 10th of this month, each of them shall take a lamb for himself according to the house of their fathers, a lamb for each household. If the household is too small for a lamb, let them share one with their neighbor who dwells next to them according to the number of people, according to what each household will eat.

READER #2 Your lamb shall be without blemish, a male of the first year. You may take it from the sheep or from the goats. You shall keep watch over it until the 14th day of this month and then the whole community will assemble and slaughter them at sunset. They shall take of the blood and put it upon the two doorposts and the lintel of the houses in which they will eat it.

READER #3 They shall eat the new that same night. They shall roast it over fire and eat unleavened bread and bitter herbs with it. It shall not be eaten raw or boiled but is to be roasted in fire - its head, legs and entrails. Nothing of it shall remain until morning. All that remains shall be burnt with fire.

READER #4 This is the manner in which you shall eat it: Your loins shall be girded; your sandals shall be upon your feet and your staff shall be in your hand. You shall eat it in haste for it is YHWH's Passover. For I will pass through the land of Egypt and strike down every firstborn in the land, both man and beast and I will execute judgment against the gods of Egypt.

READER #5 The blood upon the house in which you are in will be a sign for you. When I see the blood - I will PASS OVER you as I strike the land of Egypt. This day shall be to you a memorial and you shall keep it as a feast to YHWH throughout your generations. You shall keep it as a feast by an ordinance forever."

The Cup of Sanctification - Sanctification = KIDDUSH (set apart for a special purpose, made holy)

READER :

"Do not be unequally yoked together with unbelievers. For what fellowship has righteousness with lawlessness? And what communion has light with darkness? And what accord has Messiah with Belial? Or what part has a believer with an unbeliever? And what agreement has the Temple of Elohim with idols? For you are the Temple of the living Elohim as YHWH has said,

I will tabernacle in them and walk in them. I will be their Elohim and they shall be My people. Therefore, come out from among them and be separate. Touch not that which is unclean and I will receive you and I will be a Father to you and you shall be My sons and daughters." - 2 Corinthians 6:14-18

Let us pray this blessing together, preparing our hearts and minds for the full meaning of this Passover celebration:

EVERYONE

You, YHWH, are our Elohim and Father - The Elohim of Abraham, Isaac and Jacob. May You be pleased with the lives we live by faith in Your Son. Sanctify us with Your Spirit, satisfy us with Your goodness, cause us to rejoice in Your salvation and purify our hearts to serve You in sincerity and truth. Amen.

Drink Cup #1

MAGGID V' YAKHATZ - The Telling and Breaking of the Bread of Affliction

Please take a piece of matzah bread. Notice its texture, color and design. The bread you hold in your hand has been sifted, beaten and pierced only to be sealed in a dark oven of torment and heat - all for our benefit.

Like this matzah, our Savior Yeshua was without leaven (sin), unjustly tried, His body was stripped and bruised with brutal beatings, His hands and feet were pierced and into His side was thrust a Roman spear. His body was then sealed in a dark tomb as His Spirit descended to the fiery depths where He took from the enemy the keys to death and hell (Hades) - all for our benefit.

AFIKOMEN

The tradition of setting aside three matzah pieces originated during the exile years when Judah was taken captive to Babylon. The rabbi's taught that it represented:

The TANAKH (Bible): Torah, Prophets and the Writings
The patriarchs: Abraham, Isaac and Jacob

For those of us under the New Covenant, we can clearly see:

YHWH - the one true and living Elohim and Father of all creation.

YHWH's Son - our Adonai and Messiah Yeshua
YHWH's Spirit (Ruakh Ha' Kodesh) - YHWH's anointing power which He pours out, fills and seals each believer with.

I will now take the middle piece of matzah and break it in half. This portion is called the "afikomen" and will be eaten at the end of our Seder meal. The other half will be wrapped and hidden, placed in a location where no eye can see.

The piece is wrapped and all eyes are closed as the afikomen is "buried."

The Cup of Judgment

A full cup symbolizes fullness of joy. The tremendous suffering of Egypt diminishes our joy as we recall the plagues of judgment and affliction YHWH was forced to use in obtaining our freedom.

Yeshua our Passover has taken this judgment for us and has now made us righteous before YHWH our Elohim.

As we recite together the ten plagues of judgment, we will diminish our cups by one drop. Each time we dip our finger, we are reminded of the finger of Elohim as He afflicted Pharaoh and his people.

Using your folded napkin to catch drops, let us dash our finger as we call out these (10) plagues:

EVERYONE:

BLOOD!
FROGS!
LICE!
SWARMS!
LIVESTOCK!
BOILS!
HAIL!
LOCUSTS!
DARKNESS!
FIRSTBORN!

DAYENU - It is Enough!

The Hebrew word "DA-YENU" refers to a condition of not just having enough of something but having all our needs met - and more.

READER #1

Yes, it would have been enough to deliver us from slavery, but YHWH gave us great wealth and made us a mighty people.

EVERYONE: DA-YENU!

READER #2

Yes, it would have been enough to provide us water, quail and manna in the desert, but YHWH gave us His holy Torah to feed us and show us how to be a separate people unto Him.

EVERYONE: DA-YENU

READER #3

Yes, it would have been enough to have animal sacrifices temporarily cover our sins, but YHWH gave us His Son who paid the price for us all - forever!

EVERYONE: DA-YENU!

READER #4

Yes, it would have been enough to YHWH dwell among our tents, but He gave us His Spirit that now dwells within us and will raise us from the dead at the resurrection!

EVERYONE: DA-YENU!

The Cup of Redemption

The word "AFIKOMEN" comes from the Greek word "IKNEOMAI" which literally means, "I HAVE COME!" Since it is eaten after the

Seder meal, it became known as the Passover "dessert." It was at this point in Yeshua's last Seder supper that He instituted the New Covenant.

READER:
And as they were eating, Yeshua took the matzah and after blessing it, He broke it, gave it to His disciples and said,

"Take and eat. For this is my body."

Then He took the cup, blessed it, and gave it to them saying,

"Drink from this, all of you. For this is My blood of the New Covenant, which is shed for many for the remission of sins." - Matthew 26:26-28

(The AFIKOMEN is shared among everyone and then raised in the air. . .)

EVERYONE:
The bread is in remembrance of the body of Yeshua that was offered as a sacrifice unto Elohim our Father.

(The cup is now raised. . .)

And the cup is in remembrance of the Blood of Yeshua that makes atonement for the sins of the world. Amen.

The Exodus Story

READER #1: The story of the Exodus begins with YA' AKOV (Jacob) who has given the name YISRA' EL (Israel) by the Angel of YHWH after they wrestled together at Peniel. One of Israel's sons, YOSEF (Joseph), who through the course of events and divine intervention, was initially imprisoned in Egypt but later came to rule the country under Pharaoh. Because of Joseph, the entire family of Israel was spared from the famine that swept throughout the land. Israel, his (12) sons and their tribes settled in Egypt's fertile area of Goshen and prospered.

READER #2: As history has shown time and time again when Elohim's people prosper, the world becomes envious and we are once again persecuted. For many years, the children of Israel grew in numbers and a new Pharaoh eventually came to rule over Egypt. Joseph had died long before the new Pharaoh came to power and the friendship between the Hebrews and Egyptians no longer existed. The Hebrews were strong in numbers and Pharaoh became fearful of losing his power over the people, therefore he changed the freedom of Israel into that of slavery.

READER #3: Over the years, each new Pharaoh continued to keep Israel in bondage, increasing their hardships and labor. A few centuries later, the reigning Pharaoh was frustrated that despite the slavery and hard labor placed on the children of Israel, they somehow continued to increase in numbers. His final solution was to slaughter every newborn male child. His order, however, was disobeyed by the midwives and Israel continued to survive.

READER #1 One of the new mothers, in a desperate act of save her son, placed him in a floating basket and sent it down the Nile River where she knew the daughter of Pharaoh would be. Once again, through divine intervention, events would play out to see this child, MOSHEH (Moses) be raised as Pharaoh's grandson, (though he knew he was himself a Hebrew) and live for forty years in safety and prosperity in Egypt.

READER #2 One day while defending one of his fellow Hebrews, Moses' misguided zeal led him to kill an Egyptian, forcing him to flee the land of Egypt. Moses found refuge in the land of Midian, far from the power of mighty Egypt's reach and there he settled, married and became a shepherd.

READER #3 At the age of 80, Moses was finally ready to be used by Elohim. The same Angel of

YHWH who wrestled with Jacob almost five hundred years before, now appeared to Moses in the form of a burning bush.

READER #1 Elohim had been known by the patriarchs only by the title of "EL SHADDAI" (Elohim of the Mountains), but through His Angel, He revealed to Moses His eternal name so that both Pharaoh and the children of Israel would know who it was that sent Moses and was demanding of Pharaoh to, "Let My people go!"

READER #2: Elohim told Moses through His Angel in the burning bush, "You shall say to the children of Israel: YHWH ELOHIM of your father, the Elohim of Abraham, the Elohim of Isaac and the Elohim of Jacob has sent me to you. This is My name forever and this is My memorial to all generations." (Exodus 3:15)

READER #3 With the support of his older brother Aaron, Moses obeyed YHWH and journeyed back to Egypt to demand Pharaoh to release the children of Israel or the Elohim of the Hebrews - YHWH - would bring upon the land insufferable plagues. Pharaoh asked, "Who is YHWH that I should obey His voice to let Israel go? I do not know YHWH, nor will I let Israel go." (Exodus 5:2)

READER #1: True to His word, YHWH poured out plague after plague on Pharaoh's people. Each plague was a humiliation and affront to a different Egyptian Elohim, demonstrating YHWH's sovereignty that He alone was the one true and all-powerful Elohim. Pharaoh retaliated against the plagues by forcing the Hebrews to not only make more bricks, but they were also forced to gather the necessary materials to make the bricks - all without decreasing their required quotas.

READER #2: Before the last plague, YHWH told Moses what the children of Israel were to do to be saved from the final judgment coming upon Egypt: A firstborn male lamb without blemish was to be sacrificed and its blood applied to the doorposts and lintels of their houses.

READER #3 The sacrifice was to be offered by fire and eaten (received) quickly. They were to be ready at a moment's notice, dressed and prepared to go. YHWH then passed over every house where the lamb's blood was applied, but for those not covered by the blood - great suffering took place.

READER #1 "And it came to pass at midnight, YHWH struck all the firstborn in the land of Egypt. From the firstborn of Pharaoh who sat on his throne to the firstborn of the captive in the dungeon and all the firstborn of the livestock. So Pharaoh, his servants and the Egyptians rose in the night and there was a great cry in Egypt - for there was not a house where one was not dead." (Exodus 12:29-30)

READER #2 Pharaoh eventually relented and let Israel go. On their way out of the cursed land, Israel was given great favor and respect among the Egyptians after witnessing what YHWH had done. They gave Israel valuable materials, clothing and riches and some Egyptians even chose to leave with the Hebrew people to become a part of the 12-tribes of Israel. (Exodus 12:38)

READER #3 Exactly 430 years, to the day, when Jacob, his (12) sons and their tribes entered Egypt as free people - their descendants, the children of Israel, left Egypt as free people. They were now stronger, richer and more powerful than their forefather Jacob was - a force to be reckoned with to which they were referred to as the "Armies of YHWH." (Exodus 12:41)

READER #1 Soon after Israel left the sin and bondage of Egypt, Pharaoh once again changed his mind and pursued after them. Israel traveled across the Sinai Peninsula and came to the shore of the eastern section of the Reed (Red) Sea, unable to escape the 600 chariots of Pharaoh, they were trapped between narrow mountain passes and rocky terrain. As Moses raised his staff and they passed through the saving waters of the Red Sea (1 Peter 3:20), they watched as Pharaoh and his army were washed away, never to hold YHWH's people in bondage - again!

The Cup of Praise/Acceptance

YHWH told Moses,

"I will take you as My people, and I will be to you Elohim and you shall know that I am YHWH your Elohim who brought you out from under the bondage of Egypt." (Exodus 6:7)

The 4th and final cup symbolizes our hope and anticipation of spending eternity in the New Jerusalem with our Father YHWH and His Son - the Lamb of Elohim - Yeshua our Savior.
Yeshua said,
"I say to you, I will not drink of this fruit of the vine from now on until that day when I drink it new with you in My Father's Kingdom." (Matthew 26:29)

EVERYONE: Blessed are You, YHWH our Elohim, King of the universe and Your Son Yeshua our Messiah. Amen.

Drink Cup #4

Yom Kippur - Day of Atonement

Yom Kippur (Day of Atonement) is the 6th if 8 Appointed Times (Moadim) and holy occasions (MIKRA'EI) of YHWH our Heavenly Father which Israel was commanded to obey, the talmidim (disciples) of Yeshua continued to obey after His resurrection and that are still obeyed by Elohim's people today. (Lev. 16:1-34, Lev. 23:26-32).

And The LORD spoke to Moses, saying, 'Now on the tenth day of this seventh month is the Day of Atonement. It shall be for you a time of holy convocation, and you shall afflict yourselves and present a food offering to The LORD. And you shall not do any work on that very day, for it is a Day of Atonement for you before The LORD you Elohim. For whoever is not afflicted on that very day shall be cut off from his people. And whoever does any work on that very day, that person I will destroy from among his people. You shall do no work. It is a statue forever throughout your generations in all your dwelling places. It shall be to you a Sabbath of solemn rest, and you shall afflict yourselves. On the ninth day of the month beginning at evening, from evening to evening shall you keep your Sabbath." Lev. 23:26-32

Celebrated on the 10th day of the 7th month of ETHANIM

YHWH made provision for His people to have their individual sins forgiven throughout the year by presenting a burnt offering to atone for their sins (Lev. 1:1 - 4:1-35). However, as a nation YHWH instituted one day as the annual atonement in which they would be reconciled and cleansed from their sins and be brought into right standing (made righteous) before Him once again.

The specific steps of the service conducted by the High Priest and the rituals involved in the ceremony were very detailed and vital for the process to be accepted by Elohim. There was no room for error in the High Priest's actions else he would have been killed in his failure to obey the precise instruction of the ceremony. With no High Priest the Children of Israel would have been denied redemption of their sins.

The atonement and forgiveness provided through the blood of Messiah is ineffective for cleansing without one first truly forgiving the transgressions and sins that others have done to them (Matt.6:14-15).

We are to hold a MIKRASH KODESH (holy convocation).

FASTING

Some translate this humbling to mean "affliction of the soul." Not eating or drinking for twenty-four to twenty-five hours, is the customary expression of this affliction. It is not a joyous occasion. Rather, there is a certain degree of seriousness. For when YHWH judges the earth you will not be rejoicing. It is said, that on the Day of Atonement YHWH's eyes roam to and fro around the earth deciding who will live and who will die. It is in fact, a set apart rehearsal for JUDGMENT DAY. Yeshua fulfilled the first 4 Appointed Times (Passover, Feast of Unleavened Bread, Feast of First Fruits, and Shavuot or Pentecost. When He returns, He will fulfill the Feast of Trumpets (the resurrection), Yom Kippur (judgment day) and Feast of Tabernacles.
The sages reflect that we are meant to feel that the natural course of life is suspended, as if we are dead, as to better embrace life. If only for one day, we can quickly be reminded how dependent we are on Him. Only Elohim's gracious provisions can satisfy our physical appetite. Likewise, only Yeshua can satiate our spiritual appetites.

The fast is so important to this day that it is also referred to as "The Day of the Fast" or simply, "The Fast."

"But when they were sick, I wore sackcloth, I afflicted myself with fasting..."
- Psalm 35:13

We are not merely to diet on this day through the process of abstaining from food. Instead, He expects us to approach this fast in humility of heart, submitting to His authority and to His amazing grace.

"Is not this the fast that I choose: to lose the bonds of wickedness, to undo the straps of the yoke, to let the oppressed go free, and to break every yoke?"- Isaiah 58:6

The "Sabbath of Sabbaths"

Another commandment that YHWH gives us during Yom Hakippurim is that we must do no work. This day is called the "Sabbath of Sabbaths." We are not to mix our typical daily routine with this very holy day. The punishment for not obeying this commandment was death! The punishment for not accepting Yeshua as your High Priest, with His blood as your covering is still death. Elohim takes this Appointed Time very seriously and He wants it to be His day alone!

Offerings

The next commandment that the Lord gives us is that we are to present Him and offering. There are to be many offerings during the day. The whole chapter of Leviticus 16 is dedicated to describing these offerings. It is also mentioned in Numbers 29:7-11.

These sacrifices are required because, during the Temple period when this feast was fully implemented, it was the only prescribed way to deal with the magnitude of Israel's transgressions, and to return access to the Father. He could not dwell in the midst of sinfulness, so an offering had to be made to atone for the people's sins before they could even enter into His Presence.

The High Priest acted as the mediator between the people and the Lord. It was no light-hearted task to be a high priest. There was much preparation involved, and a lot of sober-minded seriousness. The Kohen Gadol, in addition to fasting, would spend much time in mental preparation for this event. There were to be no mistakes made.

Aaron, the first High Priest, was given a warning. His instructions were that he was not to enter into the Holy of Holies, except on the day of Yom Kippur, or he would face the punishment of death. Inside this most holy place were the Ark of the Covenant and the Mercy Seat. Above this was the Shechinah Glory, weighty and visible presence of The Lord.

"But He said, 'You cannot see My face, for man shall not see Me and live!"
- Exodus 33:20

The order of the High Priest's duties has been passed down through the centuries and is reflected in the order of service used today within traditional synagogues.

SYMBOLISM EXPLAINED

The reason YHWH instructed that sacrifices had to be made was to provide for the occasion for the sins of the nation to be "covered," so-to-speak, from YHWH's eyes. For this reason, the lid of the ark was named the Mercy Seat. The Mercy Seat was the seat (or throne) of atonement.

When on came in faith, with the atonement that Elohim had prescribed, only then could He display His mercy. This all prefigured the atonement that would be provided by Yeshua. Examining what the Levites did in the Tabernacle helps us to comprehend this concept. As mentioned earlier, Leviticus 17:11

tells us that the "life of the animal is in the blood" and that it was given to us, on the altar, to make atonement for our sings.

THE HIGH PRIEST

Before atoning for the sins of the people, the High Priest had to make atonement for his own sins. Even the High Priest Aaron was not above the need to cleanse himself and his family first before any redemption of the people could take place. He brought a young bull for a sin offering and a ram for the burnt offering. Before the blood could be applied to the altar, Aaron donned himself in special linen garments. These did not include the outer garments he would normally wear on other days. Only on Yom Kippur did the High Priest communicate with the Lord, in His very presence, in front of the Mercy Seat, and he did so in humility.

The High Priest was to sacrifice two young goats for a sin offering and a ram for a burnt offering. The two goats were brought before the door of the Tabernacle. Lots were cast to determine which goat would be the one designated for the sacrifice, called "chatat," and which goat would be the scapegoat, called "azazel," to be led away to die in the wilderness.

He then sprinkled the blood from the sacrificed goat, chosen by the casting of lots, onto the Mercy Seat. The blood of both the ram and the goat were sprinkle onto the Mercy Seat. This act made atonement for the Holy of Holies, the Tabernacle, and the altar itself. Even these inanimate objects had to be atoned for because they had become tainted by the nearby presence of sinful people.

After these acts had been performed, the highlight of the Yom Kippur service occurred - the ceremony of the scapegoat. (This was the goat that was not immediately sacrificed during the casting of the lots.)

"And Aaron shall lay both his hands on the head of the live goat and confess over it all the iniquities of the people of Israel, and all their transgression, all their sins. And he shall put them on the head of the goat and send it away into the wilderness by the hand of a man who is in readiness. The goat shall bear all their iniquities on itself to a remote area, and he shall let the goat go free in the wilderness."
- Leviticus 16:21-22

The High Priest would lay his hands on the animal, and this would symbolically transfer the sins of the people onto the scapegoat. This is the substitute sacrifice, or "AKEIDAH," as mentioned in the story of the "binding of Isaac," traditionally read on Yom Teruah.

THE GOATS

The two goats were considered as one offering. The slaughtered goat showed the congregation that YHWH's wrath was appeased, that their sins were covered. The live goat or scapegoat was sent into the wilderness bearing the sins of Israel and showing the congregation that their sins had been removed.

Each year the sacrifices had to be offered again and again. This is in bold contrast to the sacrifice of Elohim's only Son, Yeshua, done once and for all.

These goats foreshadowed the effect of Yeshua's sacrifice. He paid the penalty of death for us as with the first slaughtered goat, covering our sins. He also gained the victory over the Adversary of our souls, who will one day be banished for all eternity, bearing all his evil deeds on his own head, as seen by the second goat, the Azazel:

"The next day he saw Yeshua coming toward him, and said, 'Behold, the Lamb of Elohim, Who takes away the sin of the world!'" – John 1:29

He was the final payment and sacrifice for sins, covering and re-moving them so that we do not have to make atonement year after year.

YOM KIPPUR IN YESHUA'S TIME

Yeshua celebrated the holiday of Yom Kippur during the time of Herod's temple. There were many striking differences during this time...

1. The Ark of the Covenant was missing. It had been carried off by the Babylonians and was never recovered (2 Kings 24:13, 2 Chronicles 36:7). The elaborate ritual was still followed for the service, minus the ark and the Mercy Seat; therefore, The Lord's presence no longer filled the Holy of Holies. One may wonder why the ceremony continued without this key element.

2.The High Priestly office had also become corrupted by this time. He would have been appointed by Rome, during the time of Herod, and won his office by treachery and bribes.

3. During the Temple period, the preparations, conduct of the sacrifices, and observance of this Holy Day was of supreme importance because all was meant to atone for all of Israel's sins. Failing to properly observe the

rituals could render the sacrifices unacceptable and void the intended atonement.

4. Because of the importance of the ceremonial cleanliness of the High Priest on this feast, great pains were taken to ensure his ceremonial cleanliness was achieved and maintained through this time. The High Priest was sequestered in the Temple from a week before Yom Kippur until the Day.

5. If, for any reason the High Priest became unclean, he became ineligible from being able to perform his duties. If, for any reason, the High Priest was unable to perform his duties, the test went to a pre-designated substitute who also maintained ritual purity.

6. It is also noteworthy that the High Priest did not conduct any Temple services other than on Yom Kippur. During the year, all his duties were faithfully practiced so that he could conduct the Yom Kippur service fully in accordance with the Law so that Israel's sins could be covered by the Yom Kippur offerings.

PARALLELS IN LIFE AND MINISTRY OF YESHUA

1. The man standing in Readiness - Lev. 12:22

After Israel had settled in the Land it became customary that this man standing in readiness was a gentile. The traditional place that this took place was on the Mount of Olives. It is interesting to note that Yeshua was handed over to the Chief priests and elders guard, but the gospel of John points out (John 18:3,12) that He was also handed over to the gentiles.

2. Two goats stood before the doorway in the tent of meeting - Lev. 16:7-8

Yeshua after He had been turned over to the gentiles stood before the people (Matt. 27:16-26). Here again as we have seen with the two goats a choice was to be made. One was to die (24b-25 for the sins of the people) the other was to be sent away.

3. The scapegoat had priestly hands laid on its head, while sins were confessed over it - Lev. 16:21

Interestingly the priests too placed their hands on Yeshua's head (Matt. 26:67). While accusing Yeshua to be a sinner, they were in reality laying their sins on Him (Matt. 26:65).

4. After the scapegoat was sent away the priest would wash his body - Lev 16:24,26

This too is what happened. After Yeshua was sent away by Pilate, he washed his hands (Matt. 27:24).

AFTER THE TEMPLE'S DESTRUCTION

When the temple was destroyed in 70 C.E. the rabbis were faced with some perplexing questions: How does one celebrate Yom Kippur without the proper place of sacrifice? How does one have Yom Kippur without the proper Atoning sacrifice? The rabbis decided to make substitutions to fill these gaps.

After the destruction of the temple animal sacrifices were not possible as Elohim had prescribed since the altar and High Priesthood were not present. The rabbis had to develop a "non-sacrificial" approach to YHWH. Moses Maimonides, an ancient sage, wrote that "repentance atones for all transgression." The synagogue ritual by itself was performed in place of the animal sacrifice. To fill the gap of the missing blood atonement the rabbis substituted the "three T's": "Tefilah," (prayer), "Teshuvah," (repentance) and "Tzedakah" (charity). While these are admirable practices, they cannot replace YHWH's plan of blood atonement.

We must know that Elohim does not change! He still requires sacrifice. Men implemented many customs and traditions to fill the gap, though much of the ritual system was done away with after Yeshua's atonement and the events of 70 AD. Judaism has developed many other elaborate methods of atonement, as recorded in various rabbinic commentaries. However, the fact remains that observant Jewish people still ache for the day when the temple will be rebuilt, and sacrifices will be restored. It pales in comparison with knowing the Highest of High Priests, the one of a different order, and not of this world. May He come quickly.

YOM KIPPUR SERVICE

Scripture Reading
Leviticus 16:1-19, 16:20-17:11
Haftarah: Isa 57:14-58:14

AMIDAH (PRAYER OF STANDING)

Leader: "Oh YHWH, open my lips, that my mouth may declare Your praise."

Leader: We sanctify Your name in the world as they sanctify it in the highest heavens, as it is written by Your prophet: "They call to each other and say...

All: Holy, holy, holy is the Lord of Hosts, the whole earth is full of His glory!"

All: Praised! Praised! Be the splendor of YHWH our Elohim everywhere it is manifested!

Leader: And in the holy writings it is said:

All: "YHWH will reign forever: your Elohim, Oh Zion, to all generations. Praise the Lord!"

Leader: In every generation, we will tell of Your greatness; and in every age we will proclaim Your holiness. Your praise will certainly never depart from our lips. For You are a great and holy Elohim and King. Blessed are You, YHWH, the Holy Elohim.

KOL NIDRE (ALL VOWS...MESSIANIC)

All: Regarding ALL of our improper vows, bonds, resolutions, promises, obligations, and oaths to Elohim which we have vowed, sworn, and bound ourselves from this Day of Atonement until the next Day of Atonement: May the Lord cause all things to work together for our good, even any and all improper vows to and/or before YHWH our Elohim, as we repent of having made them. By His great mercy shall they be absolved, released, annulled, made void, and of no effect: they shall not be bonds, and oaths shall not be oaths.

KADDISH (SANCTIFICATION)

Leader: Let His name be glorified and sanctified throughout the universe which He created according to His purpose. May He bring about the reign of His kingdom in your lifetime, in your days, and in the lifetime of all the House of Israel, speedily and soon! And let all say, 'Amen!'

All: Let His great name be praised forever and ever, eternally!

Leader: Blessed and praised, glorified and exalted, extolled and honored, magnified and lauded be the name of the Holy One, blessed be He, although He is far greater than all blessings, hymns, praises, and songs which are offered in the world. And let all say, 'Amen!'

All: Let His great name be praised forever and ever, eternally!

Leader: May the prayers and supplication of all Israel be accepted by their Father Who is in heaven. And let all say, 'Amen!'

All: Let His great name be praised forever and ever, eternally!

Leader: May there be abundant peace from heaven, and life for us and for all Israel. And let all say, 'Amen!'

All: Let His great name be praised forever and ever, eternally!

Leader: May He Who makes peace in His high places make peace for us and for all Israel. And let all say, 'Amen!'

PRAYER FOR YOM KIPPUR

Heavenly Father, Almighty YHWH,
YHWH through Your abundant grace I will enter Your House. In awe I will bow down toward Your Holy Sanctuary. I bend the knee before YHWH my Maker.

These are trying time. My resolve has been tested. My heart is pained within me, and the fears of death have fallen upon me. For I know my transgressions, and my sin is ever before me. Against You, You alone, I have sinned, and done evil in Your eyes.

Forgive me YHWH Most High. In the Name
of Yeshua, I ask this. Almighty YHWH, my
heart is broken. Every day is a struggle. I've
sought You with everything I have.

Forgive me O Elohim, for I have erred.
Pardon me My Eternal King, for I have
intentionally sinned. For You pardon and
forgive. Blessed are You, O YHWH, the
merciful One Who pardons abundantly.
In the Name of Yeshua, I pray. Amen.

1) What does the Hebrew words MIKRASH
KODESH mean?

_____
_____
_____
_____
_____

2) Write Colossians 3:13 in the space below.
Write Matthew 6:14-15 beneath that. How are
these Scriptures similar?

_____
_____
_____
_____
_____
_____
_____
_____

3) Read Psalm 35:13. Review the paragraph about fasting in this chapter. Why is fasting referred to as "affliction of the soul"?

_____

_____

_____

_____

_____

_____

_____

4) Why - of all the Appointed Times - is Yom Kippur perhaps the most somber? What does Yom Kippur represent?

_____

_____

_____

_____

_____

_____

_____

5) What Appointed Times will Yeshua fulfill when He returns?

_____

_____

_____

_____

_____

_____

6) Why is Yom Kippur referred to as "The Sabbath of Sabbaths"? What was the punishment for working on Yom Kippur during the Temple period? What is the punishment for not accepting Yeshua as your High Priest, with His Blood as your covering?

_____

_____

_____

_____

_____

_____

7) The High Priest acted as the mediator between the people and who?

_____

_____

_____

_____

_____

8) Who was the first High Priest?

_____

_____

_____

_____

_____

_____

_____

_____

_____

9) What was the reason that YHWH instructed that sacrifices had to be made?

_____

_____

_____

_____

_____

_____

_____

_____

10) Leviticus 17:11 tells us that the "life of the animal was in the blood." Explain why these sacrifices foreshadowed the Atonement that would be provided by Yeshua:

_____

_____

_____

_____

_____

_____

_____

_____

11) What was the name of the "lid of the ark of the covenant"?

_____

_____

_____

_____

_____

12) How did they determine which goat would be the "sacrifice" and which goat would be the "scapegoat"?

_____
_____
_____
_____
_____

13) Define the Hebrew word "AKEIDAH"?

_____
_____
_____
_____
_____

14) Why would the High Priest lay his hands on the scapegoat?

_____
_____
_____
_____
_____

15) Read Matt 27:16-26. In this Scripture, the Priests placed their hands on Yeshua's head. How does this parallel the laying of hands on the goat during the Temple period?

_____
_____
_____
_____

BLESSING FOR THE SHOFAR

The shofar is our ancient, animalistic alarm clock. Hearing it tells us to wake up and it's a mitzvah, a commandment to hear its call. We say the first blessing before the shofar is sounded, then we say shehecheyanu, the blessing for milestones, to mark the occasion.

Baruch ata Adonai Eloheinu melekh ha-olam asher kidshanu b'mitzvotav v'tzivanu lishmoa kol shofar.
Blessed are You, Adonai our Elohim, Ruler of the universe, who has made us holy with commandments, and who has commanded us to hear the voice of the shofar.
Baruch ata Adonai Eloheinu melekh ha-olam shehecheyanu v'kiyimanu v'higiyanu lazman ha-zeh.
Blessed are You, Adonai our Elohim, Ruler of the universe, for giving us life, for sustaining us, and for enabling us to reach this season.

Kindling of the lights

Blessed are You, YHWH our Elohim, King of the universe, Who has sanctified us by Your Spirit and given us Yeshua our Messiah who commanded us to be the light of the world. Amen.

BA-ROOKH A-TA, YHWH ELO-HAY-NOO, MEH-LEKH HA-OLAM, AH-SHER KEED-SHA-NOO BUH-ROO-AKH-KHA VUH-NA-TAHN LA-NOO EHT YESHUA MUS-SHEE-KHAY-NUU, VUH-TZEE-VANOO LUH-HEE-OT OR LA-OLAM. AH-MAYN.

Opening Blessing

Let all the House of Israel be assured and know that Elohim has made Yeshua both Adonai and Messiah.

For He is the Way, the Truth, and the Life and no one comes to the Father except through Him.

Blessed are You, YHWH our Elohim, King of the universe and Your Son Yeshua our Messiah. Amen.

BA-ROOKH A-TA, YHWH ELO-HAY-NOO MEH-LEKH HA-OLAM, OO-VEEN-KHA YESHUA, MUH-SHEE-KHAY-NOO. AH-MAYN.

Blessing of Messiah

Blessed are You, YHWH our Elohim, King of the universe, Who has given us the way of salvation in Messiah Yeshua our Lord. Amen.

BA-ROOKH A-TA YHWH ELO-HAY-NOO, MEH-LEKH HA-OLAM AH-SHER NA-TAHN LA-NOO EHT DEH-REKH HA-YUH-SHOO-AH BUH-MA-SHEE-AKH YESHUA AH-DONAY-NOO. AH-MAYN.

Mah Tovu

How lovely are your tents, O Jacob and your dwelling places, O Yisrael.

MA TO-VOO O-HA-LEKHA YA-AH-KOV MESH-K' NO-TEKHA YES-RA-AL.

MA TO-VOO O-HA-LEKHA YA-AH-KOV MESH-K' NO-TEKHA YES-RA-AL.

VA-ANE B' ROV KHAS-D' KHA, A-VO VA-TEKHA.

ESH-TA-KH' VEH EL HA-KHOL - KAD-SH' KHA B' YER-ATEKHA.

Shema

SHEMA (Deuteronomy 6:4-9, Leviticus 19:18, Matthew 22:36-40, Mark 12:28-34)

Yeshua taught there were none greater than these two commandments and all the writings of the Torah and the Prophets are based upon these two commandments alone.

SH' MA, YISRAEL: YHWH EH-LO-HAY-NOO, YHWH EH-CHAD! BA-ROOKH SHEM K'VODE MALKHOOT-TO L' OLAM VAED.

Hear, O' Israel: YHWH is our Elohim, YHWH is one. Blessed is the name of His glorious kingdom for all eternity.

Leader: V' AHAV-TA AYT YHWH ELO-HEKHA, B'KHOL L'VAV-KHA OOV-KHOL NAF-SH'KHA, OOV-KHOL M'ODEKHA.

All: AND YOU SHALL LOVE YHWH YOUR ELOHIM WITH ALL YOUR HEART, WITH ALL YOUR SOUL AND WITH ALL YOUR STRENGTH.

Leader: V'HA-YOO HA-D'VAREEM HA-AYLEH ASHER ANOKHEE M'TSAV'KHA HA-YOM, ALL L'VA-VEKHA.

All: AND HAVE THESE WORDS WHICH I GIVE YOU THIS DAY BE UPON YOUR HEART.

Leader: V'SHENAN-TAM L'VA-NEKHA,
All: AND YOU SHALL TEACH THEM TO YOUR CHILDREN,

Leader: V'DEEBAR-TA BAM B'SHEEV-T'KHA B'VAY-TEKHA,

All: AND SPEAK OF THEM WHEN YOU SIT IN YOUR HOUSE,

Leader: OOV-LEKH-T'KHA VA-DEREKH, OOV-SHAKH-B'KHA, OOV-KOO-MEKHA.

All: AND WHEN YOU WALK ON THE WAY, WHEN YOU LIE DOWN AND WHEN YOU ARISE.

Leader: OOK-SHAR-TAM L'OT ALL YA-DEKHA, V'HI-OO L'TOTAFOT BAYN AY-NEKHA,

All: AND YOU SHALL BIND THEM AS A SIGN UPON YOUR HAND AND THEY SHALL BE BANDS BETWEEN YOUR EYES.

Leader: OOKH-TAV-TAM ALL M'ZOO-ZOT BAY-TEKHA OO-VEESH-AREKHA.

All: AND YOU SHALL WRITE THEM UPON THE DOORPOSTS OF YOUR HOUSE AND ON YOUR GATES.

And the 2nd greatest Commandment is this:

Leader: V'AHAV-TA L'RAY-AKHA KAMOKHA.

All: AND YOU SHALL LOVE YOUR NEIGHBOR AS YOURSELF.

Mam'lekhet Kohanim (Royal Priesthood)

LEADER: Blessed are You, YHWH our Elohim, King of the universe and Your Son Yeshua our Messiah, through whose blood You have established Your New Covenant and have made Him our Lord and High Priest.

GROUP: Through HIs resurrection You have made us a Royal Priesthood and a chosen generation.

LEADER: As royalty, You have appointed us thrones upon which we will reign together as kings with Yeshua after the earth has been renewed.

GROUP: As priests, You have appointed us as ministers of Your good news to the nations outside your covenant.

LEADER: Just as You required Your priests of the older covenant to be born only into one household to be washed in water and anointed with Your holy oil,

GROUP: So also You have required Your newer covenant priests to be born into only one family household to be washed in water and anointed with Your Holy Spirit.

LEADER: Yeshua our High Priest stated "unless one is born of water and spirit, they cannot enter into the Kingdom of Elohim".

GROUP: You, YHWH, have saved us in your mercy through the washing of our rebirth into Your family and the renewing of our inner man by the anointing of Your Holy Spirit.

LEADER: By repenting of our sins, being washed in water in the name of Yeshua, and being born of Elohim's Spirit by believing that Yeshua is the Messiah,

GROUP: We have been born anew into the family of Elohim of the Household of Yisra'el, becoming partakers of the heavenly calling within the royal priesthood of the new covenant.

LEADER: Therefore, as priests of the new covenant, let us always remember that YHWH is not unjust to forget our work and labor of love which we have shown toward His Son's name.

GROUP: Through our faith and diligence in ministering to the elect of Elohim and teaching the Good News of Messiah to all the nations outside the covenant, let us stay steadfast in our hope and faith that they, too, will choose to be born again and enter into and remain in the House of Israel to be saved.

Hodu (Give Thanks)

This song is based on Psalm 136.

Give thanks to the Lord, He is good. His mercy forever endures. Give thanks to the Lord, He is go-oo-od. His mercy forever endures.

HO-DOO LADONI KE TOV, KE LE-O-LAM
KHAS-DO
HO-DOO LADONI KE TOV, KE LE-O-LAM
KHAS-DO

HO-DOO, HO-DOO - HO-DOO, HO-DOO - HO-
DOO LADONI KE TOV
HO-DOO, HO-DOO - HO-DOO, HO-DOO - HO-
DOO LADONI KE TOV

L'kha Dodi (Come my beloved)

LUH-KHA DO-DEE, LEEK-RAHT KA-LA PUH-
NAY SHABAT NUH-KAB-LAH.
LUH-KHA DO-DEE LEEK-RAHT KA-LA PUH-
NAY SHABAT NUH-KAB-LAH.

SHA-MOR VUH-ZA-KHOR BUH-DEE-BOR EH-
KHAD HEESH-MEE-ANOO AYL HAM-YOO-
KHAD. YHWH EH-KHAD OO-SHEHMO EH-
KHAD LUH-SHAYM OOL-TEEF-ERET VUH-
LEET-HEH-LAH.

LUH-KHA DO-DEE, LEEK-RAHT KA-LA PUH-
NAY SHABAT NUH-KAB-LAH.
LUH-KHA DO-DEE, LEEK-RAHT KA-LA PUH-
NAY SHABAT NUH-KAB-LAH.

HEET-NA-AREE MAY-AFAR KOO-MEE! LEEV-
SHEE BEEG-DAY TEEF-AR-TAYKH, AH-MEE
AL YAD BEN YEE-SHAI BAYT-HA-LAKH-MEE.
KAR-VA EL NAF-SHEE GUH-ALA.

LUH-KHA DO-DEE, LEEK-RAHT KA-LA PUH-
NAY SHABAT NUH-KAB-LAH.
LUH-KHA DO-DEE, LEEK-RAHT KA-LA PUH-
NAY SHABAT NUH-KAB-LAH.

HEET-OR-REE, HEET-OR-REE! KEE VAH O-
RAYKH KOO-MEE O-REE. OO-REE, OO-REE
SHEER DA-BAY-REE KEE KUH-VOD YHWH
ALAI-YEEKH NEEG-LAH!

LUH-KHA DO-DEE, LEEK-RAHT KA-LA PUH-NAY SHABAT NUH-KAB-LAH.
LUH-KHA DO-DEE, LEEK-RAHT KA-LA PUH-NAY SHABAT NUH-KAB-LAH.

GROUP: Come, my beloved, to welcome the bride, the presence of Shabbat we receive.

READER 1: In one divine utterance "Observe and Remember" when we heard from the one and only Elohim. YHWH is one and His name one, for renown, for splendor, and for praise.

GROUP: Come, my beloved, to welcome the bride, the presence of Shabbat we receive.

READER 2: Shake off the dust, arise! Dress in garments of glory, my people, through the son of Jesse, the Bethlehemite redemption draws near to my soul.

GROUP: Come, my beloved, to welcome the bride, the presence of Shabbat we receive.

READER 3: Wake up, wake up! For your light has come! Awaken, awaken, sing a song, for the glory of YHWH is revealed to you!

GROUP: Come, my beloved, to welcome the bride, the presence of Shabbat we receive.

AMIDAH (PRAYER OF STANDING)

AMIDAH (Shemoneh Esreh)

This prayer is commonly referred to as the "AMIDAH", meaning "standing," as it reflects showing reverence by standing before YHWH our Elohim, our King, as He sits upon His throne in heaven.

Tradition calls for the Amidah to be said while facing Jerusalem with both feet together like the angels depicted in Ezekiel 1:7. It is customary to read the Amidah quietly to oneself and focus on a deeper sense of holiness (KAVVANAH) of mind while saying the words.

In ancient fashion of coming before a king, it is customary to take three small forward steps before reciting the prayer and then three steps backward at its completion. The sentence, "OSEH SHALOM BIMROMAV" (He who makes peace in His heights . . .), is then said while the person slightly bows three times from the waist: towards the left, the right and then forward.

The Amidah is called "Shemoneh Esreh" meaning "eighteen" as the original version consisted of eighteen blessings. It is also referred to as, TEFILLAH (The Prayer) as it was the entire conception of prayer itself containing praise, confession, petition and thanks.

Leader: "Oh YHWH, open my lips, that my mouth may declare Your praise."

Leader: We sanctify Your name in the world as they sanctify it in the highest heavens, as it is written by Your prophet: "They call to each other and say;

All: Holy, holy, holy is the Lord of Hosts, the whole earth is full of His glory!"

All: Praised! Praised! Be the splendor of YHWH our Elohim everywhere it is manifested!

Leader: And in the holy writings it is said:

All: "YHWH will reign forever: your Elohim, Oh Zion, to all generations. Praise the Lord!"

Leader: In every generation, we will tell of Your greatness; and in every age we will proclaim Your holiness. Your praise will certainly never depart from our lips. For You are a great and holy Elohim and King. Blessed are You, YHWH, the Holy Elohim.

AVOT: The Elohim of Our Fathers

Heavenly Father, Most High Elohim,
Blessed are You, YHWH our Elohim, Elohim of our fathers, the Elohim of Avraham, the Elohim of Yitzhak and the Elohim of Ya' akov. You are our great, mighty and awesome Elohim, the Most High Who bestows loving kindness. You are the Creator of all things Who remembers the good deeds of our forefathers and in love have brought forth Your Son as the Redeemer

to their children's children for Your name's sake in love. King, Helper, Savior and Shield. Blessed are You, YHWH, Shield of Avraham. In the Name of Yeshua, I pray. Amen.

GEVUOT: The Might of Elohim

My Glorious Father in heaven,
You, YHWH, are mighty forever. By Your Spirit You raise the dead. Through Your Son You provide atonement. You cause the wind to blow and rain to fall. You sustain the living with loving-kindness, revive the dead with great mercy, support the fallen, heal the sick, set free the captives and keep faith with those who sleep in the dust. Who is like You Who does such mighty deeds? No other Elohim resembles You, our Father, our King. Who alone has power to put to death, restore life, revive the dead, and bring salvation to Your people. Blessed are You, YHWH, Who brings forth life and raises the dead. In the Name of Yeshua, I pray. Amen.

BINAH: Understanding and Insight

Heavenly Father of Forever, Sovereign YHWH,
You favor men with knowledge and teach humanity understanding. Favor us, now, with knowledge, understanding and insight that only comes from You. Blessed are You, YHWH, our Giver of knowledge and understanding. In the Name of Yeshua, we pray. Amen.

TESHUVAH: Repentance

Heavenly Father, Almighty YHWH,
Bring us back, YHWH, to Your Torah and draw us near to Your Spirit. Cause us to return to You in perfect repentance with a sincere and circumcised heart. Blessed are You, YHWH, Who delights in true repentance. In the Name of Yeshua, I pray. Amen

S' LIKHAH: Forgiveness

Heavenly Father,
Forgive us, O YHWH, for we have sinned. Pardon us, O' King, for we have transgressed Your Torah. You are our gracious Father Who pardons and forgives us in mercy and in grace. Blessed are You, YHWH, Who remits the sins of Israel by the blood of Your Lamb. In the Name of Yeshua, I pray. Amen.

GEULAH: Redemption

Yeshua, our Eternal King,
Look upon our affliction, Yeshua our Adonai, and plead our cause to Elohim our Father. Redeem us speedily for Your name's sake, for You are YHWH's Mighty Redeemer. By Your stripes and wounds we are healed. By Your blood we are cleansed and made pure. Blessed are You, Yeshua our Messiah, Redeemer of Israel. In Your Name we pray, Amen.

REFUAH: Healing

Almighty YHWH, Most High Elohim,
Heal us, O YHWH, and we will be healed. Save us and we will be saved. For You are our praise. Grant a perfect healing to all our ailments, for You are our faithful and merciful healer. Blessed are You, YHWH, Healer of Israel. In the Name of Yeshua, we pray. Amen.

BIRKAT HA' SHANIM: Prosperity for the Year

Heavenly Father,
Bless this year for us, O YHWH, in bounty. Bestow dew and rain for a blessing upon the face of the earth and increase the fruit of our labor and work of our hands. Satisfy us with Your goodness, and bless this year as the best of years. Blessed are You, YHWH, Who blesses the increase of His people Israel. In the Name of Yeshua, we pray. Amen.

KIBBUTZ GALUYOT: The Ingathering

Sovereign YHWH, Elohim of angel armies,
Let the great shofar of our freedom sound for the return of Messiah is near! Raise the banner to gather our exiles from the four corners of the earth. Blessed are You, YHWH, Who gathers His dispersed people into their Promised Land and His redeemed in the Day of the Resurrection. In the Name of Yeshua, we pray. Amen.

BIRKAT HA' MISHPAT: Restoration of Justice

YHWH Most High,
Restore our judges as in former times, our counselors as in the beginning and remove from us our sorrow and sighing. Reign over us, O YHWH, with loving kindness and compassion, and clear us from all judgment and condemnation from our past sins. Blessed are You, YHWH, Who loves righteousness and justice. In the Name of Yeshua, we pray. Amen.

BIRKAT HA' MINIM: Vengeance against the wicked

Heavenly Father, Sovereign YHWH,
Let there be no hope for those who slander You, Your Messiah of Your people, and let all wickedness perish in an instant. May all Your enemies quickly be cut down in Your wrath, and may You soon in our day uproot, crush, cast down and humble the dominion of the arrogant. Blessed are You, YHWH, Who alone will execute vengeance, destroy our adversary and humble the children of pride. In the Name of Yeshua, we pray. Amen.

BIRKAT HA' TZADIKIM: The Righteous and the Converted

My Loving Heavenly Father,
May Your compassion be stirred, O YHWH, towards the righteous, the pious, and the elders

of Your people from the House of Israel. May You be gracious towards those of the House of Judah who have been grafted into the one true Olive Tree of Israel. Grant a good reward to all who trust in Your Son's name setting our lot with them forever so that we may never be put to shame. Blessed are You, YHWH, the support and column of strength for the righteous of Your Renewed Covenant.

BIRKAT YERUSHALAYIM: The Rebuilding of the Temple

Heavenly Father, Almighty YHWH,
Return again, soon in mercy to Jerusalem Your city and dwell within it as You have promised to Your people. Rebuild, Heavenly Father, Your Holy Temple soon in our day. Cleanse this earth, quickly establish the seat of David and enthrone Your Son Yeshua as our King and Messiah. Blessed are You, YHWH, Who will rebuild the Temple in these last days. In the Name of Yeshua, I pray. Amen.

BIRKAT DAVID

Heavenly Father,
Speedily return the offspring of Your servant David, Yeshua Messiah, to reign. Let Him be exalted by Your saving power for we longingly wait for Your salvation. May His return be swift with vengeance against those who reject Your Torah and may His reign be in our days. In that

day, there shall be one Adonai and His Name shall be one. Blessed are You, YHWH, Who will cause Your Son Yeshua to reign as King over all the earth.   In the Name of Yeshua, I pray. Amen.

TEFILLAH: Answering of Prayer
Almighty YHWH,
Hear our voice, O YHWH, our Elohim, spare us and have pity on us. Accept our prayers in mercy and grace, for You are our Heavenly Father Who hears our supplications and answers them in Your perfect time. Help us not to quench Your Spirit and drive Your presence from us so that You turn Your face away and we forever perish. You hear the prayers of Your people Israel with compassion, those who have faith in Your Son Yeshua and keep Your Torah. Blessed are You, YHWH, Who hears the prayers of Your people of the House of Israel.   In the Name of Yeshua, we pray. Amen.

AVODAH: Restoration of Temple Service
My Glorious Father in heaven, YHWH Most High,
Be pleased, YHWH our Elohim, with Your people Israel and with their prayers. Restore the service to the inner sanctuary of Your Temple, and receive in love and with favor the offerings by fire of Israel with their prayers in the last days before the Tribulation. May the

worship of Your people Israel be acceptable to You and let our eyes behold the soon return of Your Messiah to Tzion. Blessed are You, YHWH, Who restores Your divine Presence to Tzion. In the Name of Yeshua, I pray. Amen.

BIRKAT SHALOM: Peace
Heavenly Father,
Grant shalom, blessing, grace, loving-kindness and mercy to us and to all Your people of the House of Israel. Bless us, Heavenly Father, one and all, with the light of Your countenance from Your Spirit which You have given to those who love and obey You. Your name and Your Word is in Your Son Yeshua through whom we have peace and the redemption of our souls. Deliver us with loving-kindness, grace and mercy and may it please You to bless Your people Israel at all times with Your shalom. Blessed are You, YHWH, Who blesses Your people of the House of Israel with everlasting shalom. In the Name of Yeshua, we pray. Amen.

BIRKAT HODA' AH: Thankfulness
Heavenly Father, Almighty YHWH,
We give thanks to You, YHWH our Elohim, the Elohim our Fathers, and to Your Son Yeshua our Messiah. Through every generation You have been the Rock of our lives and the Shield of our salvation. We will give thanks and

declare Your praise! We commit our lives into Your hands and our souls we entrust to You.

Daily Your miracles are with us. Your wonders and blessings are with us at all times, evening, morning, and noon. Because your mercies are everlasting and Your loving-kindness never ceases, we will continue to put our hope in You. Let everything that has breath, praise the name of "YESHUA," to the glory of our Heavenly Father YHWH. Blessed are You, YHWH, to Whom we give thanks and praise for the countless blessings for which we have received. In the Name of Yeshua, we pray. Amen.

Oseh Shalom (He Who makes peace)

He Who makes peace in His heights, may He
make peace upon us and upon all Israel. Now
say: Amen!

O-SAY SHALOM BEEM-RO-MAV HOO YA-AH-
SAY SHALOM AH-LAY-NOO VUH-AL KOL
YEES-RA-AYL. VUH-EEM-ROO VUH-EEM-
ROO AH-MAYN.

YA-AH-SAY SHALOM, YA-AH-SAY SHALOM,
SHALOM AH-LAY-NOO VUH-AL KOL YEES-
RA-AYL.
YA-AH-SAY SHALOM, YA-AH-SAY SHALOM,
SHALOM AH-LAY-NOO VUH-AL KOL YEES-
RA-AYL. VUH-EEM-ROO, VUH-EEM-ROO AH-
MAYN.

Kiddush
(Separateness of
the Shabbat)

V' SHAMRU (Exodus 31:16-17) (Isaiah 66:23)

The KIDDUSH blessing declares the completion of the 6th day of creation and the separateness of the SHABBAT when Elohim ceased from creating. This blessing is traditionally said over a cup of wine and begins the celebration of the sanctity and holiness of the SHABBAT as we recite, "Blessed are You, YHWH our Elohim, King of the universe, Who creates the fruit of the vine."

The Children of Yisrael shall keep the Shabbat, observing it throughout their generations as an everlasting covenant. It is a sign between YHWH and the Children of Yisrael forever. For in six days He made the heavens and the earth and on the seventh day He rested.

"And it shall come to pass, that from one new moon to another, and from one Shabbat to another, all flesh shall come to worship before Me," says YHWH.

YHWH will establish you as a holy people unto Himself just as He has sworn to you IF you keep the commandments of YHWH your Elohim and walk in His ways.

Blessed are You, YHWH, Who makes holy the Shabbat and Your people of the House of Yisrael.

The Children of Yisra'el shall keep the Sabbath, observing it throughout their generations as an everlasting covenant. It is a sign between YHWH and the Children of Yisra'el forever. For in six days He made the heavens and the earth and on the seventh day He rested.

VUH-SHAM-ROO VUH-NAY YEES-RA-AYL ET HA-SHABAT, LA-ASOT ET HA-SHABAT LUH-DO-ROTAM BUH-REET O-LAHM. BAY-NEE OO-VAYN BUH-NAY YEES-RA-AYL, OT HEE LUH-O-LAHM KEE SHAY-SHET YA-MEEM AH-SA YHWH ET HA-SHA-MAI-EEM VUH-ET HA-AH-RETZ, OO-VAI-YOM HASH-VEE-EE SHA-VAHT VA-YEE-NA-FASH.

Prayer for welcoming the Sabbath

Heavenly Father, Almighty YHWH,

Blessed are You, O YHWH my Elohim, king of the universe. May Your great Name be blessed forever and to eternity. Elohim of Abraham, Elohim of Isaac, Elohim of Jacob; who bestows kindness, who creates all things, blessed be Your Name forever.

Exalted and hallowed be Your great Name, O YHWH. Elohim of thanksgiving, master of wonders, You are the giver of life. According to Your great mercy, please forgive me of all of my sins and cleanse them away with the Holy Blood of Your Son Yeshua.

May this Shabbat be a pleasing one to You, Most High Elohim. You are eternally mighty, O Adonai YHWH, great in salvation. Who is comparable to You, O YHWH Most High? For You sustain the living with grace, You resurrect the dead with great mercy. You are an Elohim who supports the fallen, heals the sick, releases the confined.

Blessed are You, O YHWH, the giver of wisdom. I call upon YHWH, the One to be praised, open my eyes that I might see wonders from Your Torah.

I bring this prayer before You, in the Name of Yeshua. Amen.

KADDISH
(SANCTIFICATION)

KADDISH (pronounced: "KA-DEESH") is a prayer of praise declaring our hope in the resurrection and the establishment of Messiah's kingdom on earth (Revelation 20:4-5). Because of its focus on YHWH's greatness and events that occur after death, the KADDISH has been a source of encouragement for those who have lost loved ones and over the centuries it has become a tradition to recite this prayer in times of mourning.

The rabbis have taught that the greatest test of a person's faith is their ability to praise Elohim in moments of grief. For those of us of the House of Israel, the KADDISH is our proclamation of praise - whether in times of prosperity or in grief - of our victory over the grave through the redemption of Messiah Yeshua's cleansing blood and the resurrection power of YHWH's Spirit (Matthew 26:28, Romans 8:11).

There are several forms of the KADDISH, differing only slightly by the inclusion of various statements which are read on certain occasions. The original format upon which all the other versions are based predates the destruction of the Second Temple in the 1st century C.E. during the time of Yeshua. The structure of the KADDISH is a standard Jewish format which is echoed in Yeshua's teaching to His Talmidim on how to pray to the Father.

Magnified and sanctified be His great name in the world which will be renewed, where He will resurrect the dead and raise them up to eternal life, where He will rebuild the city of Jerusalem and complete His Temple within it and uproot foreign worship from the earth, where He will return the service of Heaven to its place and where the Holy One of Elohim, our Messiah, blessed is He, will reign in His sovereignty and splendor, in your lifetime and in your days, and in the lifetime of the whole House of Israel, even swiftly and soon - and say Amen. (Amen!)

Let His great name be blessed forever and to all eternity.

Blessed, praised, glorified, exalted, extolled, mighty, magnified and lauded be the name of Yeshua, blessed is He, above any blessing and song, praise and consolation that are uttered in the world - any say Amen. (Amen!)

May He who makes peaces in His high places make peace upon us and all of Israel - and again say Amen. (Amen!)

Leader: Let His name be glorified and sanctified throughout the universe which He created according to His purpose. May He bring about the reign of His kingdom in your lifetime, in your days, and in the lifetime of all the House of Israel, speedily and soon! And let all say, 'Amen!'

All: Let His great name be praised forever and ever, eternally!

Leader: Blessed and praised, glorified and exalted, extolled and honored, magnified and lauded be the name of the Holy One, blessed be He, although He is far greater than all blessings, hymns, praises, and songs which are offered in the world. And let all say, 'Amen!'

All: Let His great name be praised forever and ever, eternally!

Leader: May the prayers and supplication of all Israel be accepted by their Father Who is in heaven. And let all say, 'Amen!'

All: Let His great name be praised forever and ever, eternally!

Leader: May there be abundant peace from heaven, and life for us and for all Israel. And let all say, 'Amen!'

All: Let His great name be praised forever and ever, eternally!

Leader: May He Who makes peace in His high places make peace for us and for all Israel. And let all say, 'Amen!'

S'udat Ha'adon (The Lord's Supper)

BA-ROOKH AH-TAH YHWH ELO-HAY-NOO MEH-LEKH HA-O-LAHM HA-MO-TZEE LE-KHEM MEEN HA-ARETZ. AH-MAYN.

Blessed are You, YHWH our Elohim, King of the universe, Who brings forth bread from the earth. Amen.

The Bread is in remembrance of the body of Yeshua that was offered as a sacrifice unto Elohim our Father. Amen.

BA-ROOKH AH-TAH YHWH ELO-HAY-NOO MEH-LEKH HA-O-LAHM BO-RAY PUH-REE HA-GAFEN. AH-MAYN.

Blessed are You, YHWH our Elohim, King of the universe, who creates the fruit of the vine. Amen.

And the cup is in remembrance of the Blood of Yeshua that makes atonement for the sins of the world. Amen.

The Aaronic Blessing

Every Shabbat concludes with the pronouncement of the Aaronic Blessing over the congregation. This commanded blessing was given by YHWH to Aaron the High Priest to bless the Children of Israel.

The blessing is said with the lands lifted up and the fingers forming the Hebrew letter "SHIN", (the first letter of the title "SHADDAI"), symbolizing the anointing and all-consuming power of YHWH's Holy Spirit.

YUH-VA-REKH-KHA   YHWH   VUH-YEESH MUH'REKHA

May YHWH bless you and keep you. Amayn.

YAH-AIR YHWH PANIVE A-LEKHA VE-KHOO-NEKHA

May YHWH make His face shine upon you and be gracious to you. Amayn.

YEE-SAW YHWH PA-NIVE A-LEKHA VUHYA-SAME LA-KHA SHALOM

May YHWH lift up His countenance upon you and give you peace. Amayn.

SHABBAT SHALOM

Tallit - Prayer Shawl

In early biblical times there was no special garment like "TALLIT" (PRONOUNCED: "TA-LEET") that we have today. Instead, the garments worn by Israelites were made with a fringe in each place where the hem came to an end, and a blue thread was incorporated into the trim bordering the hem. This was a symbol of Israel's designation as a kingdom of priests, intended not so that others would recognize their position, but so that they themselves would be conscious of whom they were and would not ignore their covenant made with Elohim.

A certain vessel descending unto him, as it had been a great sheet knit at the four corners, and let down to the earth.
- Acts 10:11

The Greek text reveals that the "vessel" or "object" being lowered by four corners is a tallit, often referred to as a prayer shawl. The Tanak frequently uses the phrase 'four corners' to symbolize the whole world. The Hebrew word "KANFOT - Corners" is also the same for the 'wings' of the angels which abound on the figures resembling human beings in Ezekiel's vision of the chariot. The tallit or prayer shawl has four corners to which the tzit tzit (zeet zeet) fringes are affixed.

And YHWH spoke to Moses saying, "Speak to the children of Israel and tell them to make tzit tzit on the corners of their garments throughout their generations, and to put a blue cord in the tzit tzit of the corners.

And the tzit tzit shall be for you to look upon it and remember all the commandments (MITZVOT) of YHWH and to do them, and not to search after your own heart and your own eyes after which you went whoring, so that you remember and do all my commandments and be holy unto your Elohim." - Num. 15:37-40

It is also commanded in Deuteronomy 22:12. The blue string is in recognition of the Messiah and the eternal atonement we have due to His crucifixion. Wearing tzit tzit serves as a constant reminder of one's covenant obligation to YHWH.

A prophecy in the Tanak speaks of the Messiah as follows:

"The Sun of Righteousness shall arise with healing in His wings - Malachi 4:2

These "wings" are "KANAPH" in Hebrew, and refer to the edge of a garment, which is the tzit. So, Yeshua wore tzit tzit.

Now a woman, having a flow of blood for twelve years, who had spent all her livelihood on physicians and could not be healed by any, came from behind and touched the border of His garment. And immediately her flow of blood stopped."
- Luke 8:43-44

The Greek word used to describe a border is "KRASPEDON" which means a fringe or tassel. In other words, she grabbed his tzit tzit that He was wearing in obedience to the Torah. Therefore, He came with healing in His tzit tzit just as was foretold by the Prophet Malachi.

It was a custom in Israel that if you could pull on the Rabbi's tzit tzit, he had to stop and talk to you. She no doubt, knew of this custom and knew that she would definitely get Him to stop.

By donning a tallit a person wraps themself in the commandments, which demonstrates his or her obedience and the protective covering which YHWH provides when we live according to His ways.

Couples sometimes get married under a Tallit and in fact, there is considerable symbolism regarding the Tallit and marriage.

;Your time was the time of love, and I spread my mantle over you and covered your nakedness. And I swore an oath to you and entered into a covenant with you, and you became Mine;" - Ezekiel 16:8

One holds his hands on the sides of the crown and says the following, before putting it on:

BLESSED BE YOU YHWH, KING OF THE UNIVERSE WHO HAS SANCTIFIED US WITH

YOUR COMMANDMENTS AND COMMANDED
US TO WEAR A TZIT TZIT.

Answer the Following Questions:

1. What did Israelites wear before the TALLIT?
What was it a symbol of?

_____
_____
_____
_____
_____

2. Read Acts 10:11. What is the "vessel" or
"object" being lowered down by four corners?

_____
_____
_____
_____

3. What does the Hebrew word "KANFOT"
mean? What does this word have to do with
Ezekiel's vision of the chariot?

_____
_____
_____
_____
_____
_____

4. Are the tzit tzit commanded? If so, what are the Scriptures?

_____
_____
_____
_____

5. What is the blue string in recognition of?

_____
_____
_____
_____

6. What Scripture in Malachi was fulfilled by Yeshua's tzit tzit?

_____
_____
_____
_____

7. What does the word "KRASPEDON" mean?

_____
_____
_____
_____

8. What was the custom in Israel regarding a Rabbi's tzit tzit?

_____
_____
_____
_____

9. By donning a Tallit what is a person doing?

_____
_____
_____
_____
_____
_____

10. Read Ezekiel 16:8. What is the symbolism regarding the Tallit and marriage? How does it involve Israel as the bride?

_____
_____
_____
_____
_____
_____

11. What does one say before putting on the Tallit?

_____
_____
_____
_____
_____
_____

KIPPAH

The head covering worn by Jewish men is called a Kippah. It is derived from the Hebrew word KAFAR which means to cover, pardon, atone.

The custom of wearing a head covering goes back to ancient times and across many cultures. In both the MISHKHAN (Tabernacle) and MIKDASH (Temple), YHWH required the priesthood to cover their heads while ministering in His Presence. THE KOHEN HA'GADOL (High Priest) was also required to wear a turban-like head covering (Exodus 28:36-39) having a golden band across the forehead with the engraved words of "KODESH L'YHWH" (Holiness to YHWH).
Wearing a covering on our heads reminds us as men that we still have someone above us in divine authority.

KIPPOT (plural) are often referred to in traditional Judaism by their Yiddish name of "Yarmulke" from the Hebrew word YAREI (to revere, fear in honor with respect) and MELUKHAH (kingship, rulership).
Wearing the KIPPAH means you are in FEAR OF THE KING.

Answer the Following Questions:

1. What is the head covering worn by Jewish men?

_____

_____

_____

_____

2. Read Exodus 28:36-39. What was required to cover the head in the presence of YHWH?

_____

_____

_____

_____

_____

3. What does wearing the KIPPAH mean?

_____

_____

_____

_____

4. What does the Hebrew word "KAFAR" mean?

_____

_____

_____

_____

Isn't all Judaism the same?

Absolutely not. Within the faith of Judaism there are different sects (groups) that differ in doctrine, scriptural interpretation and application. Today, Judaism has the following five primary sects:

Hasidic - Ultra-orthodox in doctrine and lifestyle. Isolationists from society in relatively small populations. Predominantly found in the State of Israel but also have various communities within large cities in the United States, Europe and Russia. They observe Torah and rabbinic law - and reject Yeshua as the Jewish Messiah.

Orthodox - Strictly adheres to rabbinic law but does interact with society. They observe Torah but reject Yahshua as the Jewish Messiah.

Conservative - Moderately adheres to rabbinic law. More lenient in observing Torah. They reject Yeshua as the Jewish Messiah.

Reform - Judaism by name only. They adhere to little or no rabbinic law and reject most all Jewish customs and traditions. More interested in social issues instead of Elohim's Word. Their liberal acceptance of sexual immorality has attracted many from today's society. Conversions to Reform Judaism are not accepted within the State of Israel for aliyah (immigrating) purposes. They reject most all

Torah, food laws and holiness standards - and they reject Yeshua as the Jewish Messiah.

Karaite - Known as "BENEI MIKRA" (Children of the Scriptures). They reject rabbinical Judaism's "Oral Law", Talmud and all other writings not divinely inspired by Elohim. They observe Torah, biblical food laws, YHWH's appointed times and holiness standards. They reject (at least for now) Yeshua as the Jewish Messiah.

Elohim

The Hebrew does not describe "Elohim" as the Creator, but rather Elohim. Elohim is actually the plural form of "El." The original Hebrew Scriptures never refer to the Creator as "Elohim." "Elohim" is a word of Teutonic origin which refers to a pagan deity. The title used in the Hebrew text to describe the Creator is Elohim. It is the plural form of El, which means "Mighty One" or "Power."

It was Elohim Who was present during Creation, and therefore Elohim Who can provide a witness to Creation.

We see in the first sentence of the Scriptures that "In the beginning Elohim Created." The Hebrew for "created" is "bara" which literally is "He Created." It is masculine singular showing that while Elohim is plural, He is masculine singular.

Since Elohim is plural, it could be argued that there were two witnesses to creation - the Father and the Son. The Son was actually the One Who Created and the purpose of this Creation is to expand the Kingdom of the Father through His Son.

Answer the Following Questions:

1. Do the original Hebrew Scripture refer to the Creator as Elohim. If not, how do they refer to Him?

_____

_____

_____

_____

2. What is the origin of the title "Elohim"?

_____

_____

_____

_____

3. What is the Hebrew word for "created"? What does this word mean?

_____

_____

_____

_____

4. Since Elohim is plural it can be argued that there were two witnesses to creation. Who are they? And what was the purpose for it being this way?

_____

_____

_____

_____

The Mikvah

The Mikvah is where the Christian doctrine of baptism derives although it did not begin with Christianity and was commanded by YHWH long before Messiah came. It was a natural thing for Israelites to do. In fact, there were hundreds of mikvahs at the Temple and it was required that a person be immersed in a mivah prior to presenting their sacrifice. The Hebrew word for baptize is TEVILA which is a full body immersion that takes place in a mikvah which comes from the passage in Genesis 1:10 when YHWH "gathered together" the waters. The mikvah is the gathering together of flowing waters. The "TEVILA" immersion is symbolic for a person going from a state of uncleanliness to cleanliness. The priests in the Temple needed to tevila regularly to ensure that they were in a state of cleanliness when they served in the Temple. Anyone going to the Temple to worship or offer sacrifices would tevila at the numerous pools outside the Temple. There are a variety of instances found in the Torah when a person was required to tevila.

The tevila is symbolic of becoming born again and is an act of going from one life to another. Being born again is not something that became popular in the seventies within the Christian religion. It is a remarkably Israelite concept that was understood to occur when one arose from the mikvah. In fact, people witnessing an immersion would often cry out

"Born Again!" when a person came up from an immersion. It was also an integral part of the Rabbinic conversion process, which, in many ways is not Scriptural, but in this sense is correct. For a gentile to complete their conversion, they were required to be immersed, or baptized, which meant that they were born again: born into a new life.

Jewish ceremonial washing rituals first originated in the book of Exodus (SHEMOT) when YHWH required the priesthood to wash with water before entering into His presence, ";that they die not." (Exodus 29:4, Exodus 30:17-21). The Torah also mandates other various washings each person had to perform to remain ceremonially clean, both men and women. Traditional public MIKVAH pools throughout Jerusalem were designed with stairs leading down into the water with corresponding stairs at the opposite end that allowed the individual to "pass through the waters" and be cleansed.

When the prophet Yahanan (John), son of Zakhar'yah (Zechariah), began preaching repentance, the people gladly received him, obeyed his message and the Yarden River became a large MIKVAH for the multitudes. From this ancient Jewish practice of immersion, various other religions invented their own water rituals (i.e., Christianity with its infant christening / sprinkling and other various non-biblical modes of "baptism", Islam with its ablutions before entering spiritual cleansing.) Unlike these newer religions, the cleansing waters of a MIKVAH have always been a normal practice for Elohim's people and Yahanan's call to repentance followed by immersion for the remission / forgiveness of sins was not something new for those who worship the Messiah.

It is important to note that the tevila must occur in "living waters" - in other words, water which is moving and ideally which contains life. These living waters refer to the Messiah. In a Scriptural marriage, a bride would enter the waters of purification prior to her wedding. These are the same waters that we are to enter when we make a confession of faith and become part of the Body of Messiah - His Bride. A bride also enters waters of separation when her niddah period has ended so that she can be reunited with her husband.

Answer the Following Questions:

1. Where is the Christian doctrine of baptism derived from?

_____

_____

_____

_____

2. What is the MIKVAH?

_____

_____

_____

3. What is a TEVILA immersion?

_____

_____

_____

4. What is the TEVILA symbolic of? What did people used to cry out during a TEVILA immersion?

_____

_____

_____

5. Read Exodus 29:4. Read Exodus 30:17-21. Describe how ceremonial washing rituals first originated.

_____

_____

_____

6. What other religions adopted versions of the TEVILA immersion?

_____

_____

_____

_____

7. It is a must that a TEVILA immersion occur where? Explain why.

_____

_____

_____

_____

8. As the Messiah's bride, explain we are to enter waters of purification before we become a part of the Body of Messiah.

_____

_____

_____

_____

So, you think you are Messianic?

Answer the following questions:

1. SUKKOT played a part in the Egyptian exodus, what was it?

_____

_____

_____

_____

2. The 8th day is BEFORE or AFTER the 1,000 year reign?

_____

_____

_____

_____

3. Define YESHUVA

_____

_____

_____

_____

4. During MIKVAH, after being immersed it was customary for those who witness the event to say what, after they were immersed?

_____

_____

_____

_____

5. The GREATER EXODUS has already taken place. TRUE or FALSE?

_____

_____

_____

_____

6. What is the GREATER EXODUS? And which Appointed time specifically involves this event?

_____
_____
_____

7. Describe the significance of the TEN DAYS OF AWE

_____
_____
_____

8. What prophecy was fulfilled when the woman with the issue of blood pulled on Yeshua's tzit tzit?

_____
_____
_____

9. The Apostles observed the Sabbath. True or False?

_____
_____
_____

10. List the five sects of Judaism

_____
_____
_____

Works Cited

Resources for Broken Road Ministries:

Yahweh's Evangelical Assembly
PO BOX 31
Atlantic, TX 75551

The House of Yahweh
PO BOX 2498
Abilene, TX 79604

Assemblies of Yahweh
PO BOX C
Bethel, PA 19507

Yahweh's Assembly in Messiah
401 N Roby Farm Rd
Rocheport, MO 65279

Todd Bennett's – Walk in the Light Series-
available on www.shemayisrael.net

Halleluyah Scriptures
PO BOX 2283
Vineland, NJ 08362-2283

Bradford Scott- wildbranch.org

Joel Richardson- The Islamic Antichrist

Rabbi Jonathan Cahn-
www.hopeoftheworld.org

Michael Rood- www.rooadawakening.tv

Monte Judah- www.lionandlambministries.org

Eddie Chumney- www.eddiechumney.com
Hebraic Heritage Ministries International -
hebroots.org

Studies in the Torah by Tim Hegg

The Laws of the Second Coming by Dr.
Stephen Jones

What is available to me from Broken Road Ministries?

The Torah Study Series Volumes 1 to 8. These are the books in order:

Volume 1

This is where it all starts. The Basics. This book explains what the Torah is. It teaches about the Sabbath. It contains several chapters: We wrestle not against flesh and blood, The measure you use, who is your neighbor, Bereshith (an-in depth analysis of the Hebrew in the book of Genesis).

Volume 2

This book teaches the Moadim (Appointed Times from Leviticus 23). Contains the following chapters: Passover (Pesach), Feast of Unleavened Bread - Khag Ha'Matzah, Shavuot - Feast of Weeks, Passover and the Feast of Unleavened Bread, The Number Seven, The Counting of the Omer, Foot Washings, Yom Teruah - Feast of Trumpets, Ten Days of Awe, Yom Kippur

- Day of Atonement, The 7th Day, Feast of Tabernacles (Sukkot), Shemini Atzeret - The 8th Day of Ingathering, Purim, Shemot (Exodus 1:1-6:1), Israel's Prophetic Spring Feasts, and a Multiple-choice Exam at the end of the book.

Volume 3

The Name (HaShem) - Is it YHWH or Yehovah? This is a compelling Bible Study which may help you if you are in pursuit of a conclusive answer.

Elohim's Servants Scourged - Will there be scourging at The White Throne Judgment. BRM takes a look at this predominantly Christian teaching.

Volume 4

Contains Torah portion studies from the Book of Exodus.

Volume 5

Contains the following chapters: Foreword 2022, Remembering Our

Redemption (Exodus 13:1-20), Lessons
from Pesach (Exodus 12:13-28), Jacob's
Feast Day Pattern, Bo (Exodus 12:29-
51), The Feast Days in the Book of
Joel, B' SHALACH "When He Sent"
(Exodus 13:21-15:18), The 7,000 Year
Plan of Elohim, The Messiah Part 2,
The Feast Days in Elijah's Story,
Renewal.

Volume 6

Contains Bible studies from Torah
portions in Genesis, Exodus, and
Leviticus.

Volume 7

Contains the following chapters:
The Blood Cries Out, TSAV "Command"
Leviticus 8:1-36/Hebrews 7:11-28,
Presenting the Firstborn, MISHPATIM
"Ordinances" Exodus 21:1-22:24, Two or
Three Witnesses, BEMIDBAR "In the
Desert" (Numbers 1:1-2:13), Elohim's
Face is Elohim's Presence, Resist
Babylon.

Volume 8

This is a book which stands against racism/antisemitism.

We all know that this picture of a milky white "Jesus" that we inherited from the Puritans of England is not an accurate depiction of Yeshua, our Messiah (simply because of where in the world He was born!)

Perhaps Yeshua was not as black as portrayed on the cover of the book. However, it serves to make a point. Why the fear of a darker skin color on our Messiah? Why the need to change His Name? What is going on here?

I knew I had to put this book together, after a rather disturbing trip to the chapel one day at an institution. At a Christian service, there broke out a question-and-answer portion to the service. A (black) man stood up (politely) and asked, "Isn't His Name really Yeshua?" The (white) speaker (a volunteer who comes in once a week) with all sincerity responded "No, His Name is Jesus."

Something is wrong with this.

We are going to explore where this DISCONNECT started; all the way back to the pioneers of Christianity (as it broke off from the Roman Catholic Church).

Siddur

Prayer Journal

For a free copy of any of these books, write to:

Broken Road Ministries
P.O. Box 780751
Orlando, FL 32878

Made in the USA
Columbia, SC
05 August 2024

39518522R00104